Sunset
Homeowner's Guide to
Wood Stoves

BY THE EDITORS OF SUNSET BOOKS AND SUNSET MAGAZINE

Lane Publishing Co.
Menlo Park, California

Wood heat: An alternative

In the widening search for alternatives to fossil fuels in home heating, a growing number of homeowners are discovering the advantages of wood: low cost and ready availability. Efficient burning of wood for household warmth is the function of the wood stove, an uncomplicated piece of equipment, old in concept, yet modern in application. Where and how to buy a stove, how to install and use it, and where and how to obtain wood are questions answered in this book.

We are grateful to the many homeowners who allowed us to photograph their wood-heated homes. Special thanks, also, to these wood burners who shared their expertise with us: Cecil Asman, West Marin Realty; M. Willis Bibbins and John L. Davies, Bow & Arrow Stove Company; Karen Booth and Paul Eis, Northwest Wood Heat; Mike Booth; Philip Browne, Embers; Ralph Buffa, King's Mountain Wood Stoves; Art Childers, Firehouse West, Inc.; Jayona Coleman and Karen Fenton, Energy Unlimited; Ed Davis and Susan Lamb, Frizelle–Enos Co., Inc.; Anne De Wolf, The Golden Flame; Chris Dyer, Greenbriar Products Inc.; Rose Foster and Dick Stucker, Fisher Stoves; Frank and Marilyn Goff, The Stove Factory; Bill Johnson, Chinook Mfg. Company; Tom Lichty, The Oregon Woodstove Company; Bob North, Energy World; Peter Parkhurst, Natural Heating Company; Mary Stiletto, The Ground Floor; Beverly S. Stone, Wood Heat, Inc.; Frank and Karen Verprauskus, Pacific Wood Stove Distributors.

Staff Editors:

Jim Barrett
Donald W. Vandervort
Scott Fitzgerrell
John McCarthy

Supervising Editor:

René Klein

Design: Mark Landstrom
Timothy Bachman
Illustrations: Dennis Nolan

Cover:

Situated near the center of the kitchen-living-dining area, this attractive stove warms them all; some of its heat is stored in the brick and tile for later release. Photographed by Jack McDowell.

Sunset Books
    Editor, David E. Clark
    Managing Editor, Elizabeth L. Hogan

Fourth printing April 1987

Contents

Special Features

Plan before You Buy

- HEATING YOUR HOME WITH WOOD
- DETERMINING YOUR HEATING NEEDS
- FINDING A STOVE THAT FILLS YOUR NEEDS
- BUYING A STOVE

Range

Cookstove

Potbelly stove

Parlor stove

Circulating heater

Barrel stove

Scandinavian stove

aking wood heat an effective
alternative to conventional heating
requires the ultimate in careful
planning. Like any major home appliance, the
wood stove or heater and its installation can
represent a sizable financial investment, and it
is crucial to select the right appliance for the job
and to position it for maximum heating efficiency.

Whether you inherit a grand antique or expect
to buy a new stove, the careful planning you do
now will pay off later.

This section will guide you from plan to
purchase. First, you'll learn about wood heat,
how wood compares to other fuels, and about the
various kinds of stoves and how they work.
Next, you'll find information on how to
determine your heating needs—a planning phase
so important it can't be stressed enough. Finally,
there is advice on making the actual purchase:
how to find a reputable dealer and how to judge
the quality of a stove.

Heating Your Home with Wood

Today's technology makes heating your home as simple as setting a thermostat. But many homeowners are finding the use of fossil fuels and electricity a costly way to heat. If wood is plentiful in your area, why not look into wood stoves and heaters as a practical solution to the rising costs of conventional heat?

Heating with wood is a positive step toward self-sufficiency; it is also a step away from some of the conveniences you now take for granted. But despite the fact that heating with wood entails some chores, it does offer pleasures.

Wood as fuel

Wood, man's first fuel, is actually stored solar energy. A tree's leaves function as tiny solar collectors to harness sunlight which the tree uses to convert water, carbon dioxide, and nutrients into organic matter—wood. One has but to light a match to release this stored solar energy.

Since the dawn of human history, man has attempted to improve the means by which he converted wood's stored energy into useful energy for heating and cooking, but his efforts got sidetracked by the advent of more efficient heating devices that use fossil fuels and electricity. As a result, little technological progress has been made in wood-burning until quite recently. Today, the interest in wood fuel as an economically feasible alternative to conventional home heating is fostering the development of more efficient woodburners.

Wood vs. conventional heating

There are, of course, advantages and disadvantages to wood heat. On the positive side, wood frees us from our reliance on the power company or fuel truck. In the event of power outages, fuel shortages, or other emergencies, it's very comforting to know that a source of heat is as close as the wood pile.

Costwise, wood is definitely competitive with fossil fuels and electricity in most parts of the country. Dwindling fossil fuel supplies and the development of more efficient wood stoves will make wood more economical compared to other fuels. The following chart will help you see just how competitive wood can be in relation to other heating fuels in your area, and it will show you which woods produce the most heat per cord. A quick look reveals that some woods have twice the heating potential of others when burned in the same way.

The figures listed are based on the efficiency of average heating units, for fuel oil, natural gas, and liquified petroleum (LP) gas. Electric heating units in theory, are virtually 100 percent efficient. A quality airtight stove, operated at maximum efficiency, should be about 60 percent efficient, though some stoves have done better than this.

These figures are meant to be used as general comparisons; actual efficiencies of various stoves and conventional heaters may differ from those shown. BTU ratings for wood species are based on the usable heat generated by a cord when burned in a 60 percent efficient stove. The figures assume that the wood has a 20 percent moisture content—considered the norm for seasoned, air-dried wood. The BTU content of green (unseasoned) wood will be considerably less.

To use the chart, check your utility bill or call your utility company to find out the cost per gallon, therm, or kilowatt hour for conventional fuels in your area. Multiply this number by the number of gallons, therms, or kilowatt hours found opposite the species of wood you are thinking of using. Now all you need is a price per cord for this wood, and you can

(Continued on page 8)

Comparative Heat Values: Wood vs. Other Fuels

Multiply cost of present fuel (per gallon, therm, or kilowatt hour) by the corresponding number on the chart opposite the wood you'll be using. Then compare against the price of a cord of the wood.

Common Fuelwoods	Usable Heat BTU's per cord[1]	No. 2 Fuel Oil (gallons)[2]	Natural Gas (therms)[3]	Electricity (KWH)[4]	LP Gas (gallons)[5]
Apple Hickory, shagbark Ironwood (hardhack) Locust, black Oak, live	14.4 million	147	180	4220	196
Dogwood Elm, rock Oak, white	13.8 million	141	173	4044	188
Birch, yellow Maple, sugar Oak, red	12.6 million	129	158	3693	171
Ash, white Eucalyptus (all species) Walnut, black	12 million	122	150	3517	163
Birch, white Cherry, black Fir, Douglas Maple, red Tamarack (Eastern larch)	11.4 million	116	143	3341	155
Ash, green Pine, pitch Sycamore, American	10.8 million	110	135	3165	147
Ash, black Elm, American Maple, silver	10.2 million	104	128	2989	139
Alder Cedar Hemlock Spruce, red	8.4 million	86	105	2462	114
Aspen (poplar) Pine, red Willow, black	7.8 million	80	98	2286	106
Basswood Fir, balsam Pine, Ponderosa Pine, sugar Pine, white Redwood	7.2 million	73	90	2110	98

1. *Seasoned wood at 20% moisture content, burned in 60% efficient stove*
2. *140,000 BTU's per gallon, burned at 70% efficiency*
3. *100,000 BTU's per therm, burned at 80% efficiency*
4. *3412 BTU's per kilowatt hour, using electric heater at 100% efficiency*
5. *92,000 BTU's per gallon, burned at 80% efficiency*

... *Continued from page 6*

see whether or not, and to what extent, wood heat is a viable alternative for you.

Money aside, there's a certain esthetic charm involved in the ritual of burning wood—the subtle smell and sounds of a fire burning inside the stove, and the uniquely sensuous warmth it radiates. The stove itself can be an attractive addition to the home —it has a way of becoming a member of the family.

But wood-burning does involve work. Wood must be gathered, seasoned, cut to stove length, and stored. You can, of course, buy your wood precut, seasoned, and delivered, but it will cost much more. Then there's the routine of loading the stove at least once a day, monkeying with the damper controls, removing the ashes on a regular basis, and cleaning the flue pipe several times a year. Unless you're a devout wood-burner, these chores can grow tiresome as the novelty of the stove wears off, but you'll need to accept them as part of your new, self-sufficient life style. It is, of course, a matter of attitude. If you've grown used to pumping your own gasoline, you'll find that tending the stove is not much more difficult.

How wood burns

To understand how wood stoves work, you should know how wood burns. In order for wood to burn, two things must be present: high temperature and oxygen. Both temperature and air supply must be maintained throughout the burning process or the fire will smolder and die. When wood burns, it goes through three phases of combustion:

1. Moisture is evaporated from the wood by the surrounding fire. All wood (unless oven or kiln-dried) contains a certain percentage of moisture. Because part of the fire's heat is used to evaporate this moisture, seasoned wood (20 percent moisture) is preferable to green or freshly cut wood (50 percent or more moisture). The first phase is complete when the wood reaches 212°F/100°C (the boiling point of water).

2. Wood breaks down chemically into volatile gases and charcoal as the temperature continues to rise. The wood "catches fire" at about 600°F/315°C, burning a small percentage of the gases and the charcoal. Most of the volatile gases, however, will escape up the flue unless the temperature inside the stove is sufficiently high to burn them (phase 3). Once in the flue, the unburned gases will combine with vaporized moisture to form creosote inside the chimney or flue pipe walls (see "Creosote," page 81).

3. Volatile gases and charcoal burn. Charcoal begins to emit heat and burn at about 1,000°F/540°C, reducing itself to ash. Called the "coaling" process, this is when wood ordinarily produces the most usable heat.

The volatile gases will ignite when they reach a temperature of 1100°F/600°C, provided they have enough oxygen supplied at the point of combustion.

The gases rarely reach this temperature unless they are restricted in some manner and rerouted over the flame of the fire or to an area where these high temperatures have been achieved. Part of a stove's heating efficiency depends on its ability to do this.

This description of the burning process is somewhat simplistic—the combustion of wood is a complex chemical process involving a number of variables. For practical purposes, though, you need only remember that in order for a stove to burn wood efficiently it must retain a high enough temperature and provide enough oxygen to burn as much of the wood and its gases as possible.

The wood stove

Once you've decided to buy a wood stove, there's still a lot of decision-making to do before you go out shopping for one. First you must determine your heating and esthetic needs; then you must decide where and how you'll install the stove to meet these needs. You'll have to consider what conveniences you want from your stove—how easy it must be to operate and maintain. Then you must decide on a price range—stoves range from around $100 to $900 or more (and don't forget to add the cost of chimney installation). Because you'll want your stove to provide many troublefree years of service, you'll have to learn to recognize quality in materials and manufacture. Once you've faced these considerations, **then** ask yourself the ultimate question: **Which stove will I buy?** The following chapters will help you make these decisions.

Kinds of stoves

In the past 10 years, the number of stoves on the market has increased more than fivefold—today there are several hundred from which to choose. Almost all of these differ somehow in design and appearance, making it difficult to place them into neat classifications. There are, however, certain characteristics held in common that make grouping possible.

First, all wood stoves and heaters fall into two general categories: airtight and nonairtight. Airtight stoves are sealed tight except for one or two adjustable air inlets (damper controls) to control the stove's burning rate. The loading doors have airtight gaskets that seal them when closed. Most modern stoves are airtight; antique stoves and their reproductions are usually not (see "Heating efficiency," page 20).

Another method of classifying stoves is by material. A few stoves are made of ceramics or soapstone, but most are made of either cast iron or steel, or a combination of the two. Both cast iron and

The Franklin fireplace: Ben's compromise

In colonial times, English settlers built massive fireplaces to ward off the severe Yankee winters. However, these fireplaces actually contributed little heat to the colonial homes and often left their occupants freezing, unless they were huddled directly in front of the open fire. Other European settlers, including the Dutch, French, Germans, and Scandinavians, survived the winters in greater comfort with their cast-iron stoves. But the English stubbornly refused to give up their "view of the fire" and their inefficient fireplaces.

By the mid 1700s most colonial homes still had these fireplaces that, in addition to being poor heaters, consumed great amounts of wood. It was during this time, when a wood shortage threatened Philadelphia, that Benjamin Franklin invented the "Pennsylvania fireplace." Both inventor and statesman, Franklin sought to provide a compromise by inventing a device that approached the efficiency of a closed cast-iron stove, yet allowed its user to see the fire . . . a consolation most Anglo-Americans would still not relinquish.

Franklin's first fireplace was actually an open stove. It consisted of cast-iron plates that formed an open box, with a shutter device on the open end to control the draft. It was designed with a false bottom and back that contained a series of air passages. These passages rerouted the rising smoke and hot flue gases behind and underneath the firebox and back through the fire, burning the gases more completely than a conventional fireplace could. Thus, Franklin's fireplace, or stove, burned wood more efficiently, and radiated additional heat from the hot flue gases before they entered the chimney. It also had an air passage that admitted outside air, heated it, and expelled it into the room.

Further improvements in Franklin's original fireplace included doors that could be opened to view the fire, or closed for greater wood-burning efficiency. Because Franklin did not believe in patents—and,

Franklin's Pennsylvania fireplace

when offered one, refused it—his Pennsylvania fireplace was widely imitated and altered in design and principle. By the mid 1800s the Franklin fireplace, or stove, had evolved to its present traditional form, which bears no resemblance in appearance or design to Ben's original. In fact, the term "Franklin" today is loosely applied to a number of stoves with doors that open to allow a view of the fire. Traditional Franklins and their counterparts appear throughout the color section, pages 32–63.

In addition to his Pennsylvania fireplace, Franklin is credited with inventing the first down-draft stove. The device was a closed stove in which combustion air entered through the top, forcing smoke and volatile gases down through the coals for more complete combustion. This stove, too, had a series of air passages that allowed the hot flue gases to transmit their heat to the stove body before going up the chimney. Though this invention may be the true Franklin stove, it did not receive such wide acclaim as his original Pennsylvania fireplace.

steel have their advantages and disadvantages, though the quality of the stove is usually determined by the thickness of these materials (see "Choosing a durable stove," page 26).

Some stoves are named for their appearance or design—potbelly stoves, box stoves, barrel stoves, for example. Scandinavian stoves, named for the area of their origin, are cast-iron, airtight box stoves with a secondary combustion chamber and baffle system to improve their efficiency.

Cookstoves and ranges are obviously named for the function they perform, though many stoves designed primarily for heating do have limited capabilities for cooking. Examples of the classic stove designs appear on page 4.

Many of the modern stoves are unique in design, though they may share some of the characteristics of those just mentioned. These stoves are often referred to by brand name only in manufacturer's literature, or may be further distinguished by model name or number in the manufacturer's line.

Stoves may also be referred to as "open stoves" or "closed stoves." Closed stoves, as their name implies, completely enclose the fire and are designed to operate with their doors shut. Some closed stoves have windows of tempered glass or mica in their doors to give you a peek at what's going on inside the stove.

Open stoves, on the other hand, have large doors that may be opened to view the fire. The Franklin stove is an example of an open stove. These stoves are much more efficient as heaters when their doors are closed, though a generous view of the fire may be worth the loss in heating efficiency on some occasions.

Some open stoves are very similar in design and appearance to some of the modern freestanding fireplaces on the market today—in fact there's little dis-

tinction between them, other than the description used by the manufacturer.

Some stoves are designed to fit inside conventional masonry fireplaces. These in-the-fireplace stoves come in sizes to fit standard fireplace openings, and they're vented directly into the fireplace chimney. Most have tempered glass or screens in their doors for fire viewing. They work on the same principle as a circulating stove (see drawing on page 12). When operating, the stove heats the air between it and the walls of the fireplace—the heated air then circulates by convection out into the room. These stoves are one good way to make a conventional fireplace more heat efficient without sacrificing the pleasure of watching the fire. Other ways of retrofitting a masonry fireplace to accept a wood stove are discussed on page 76.

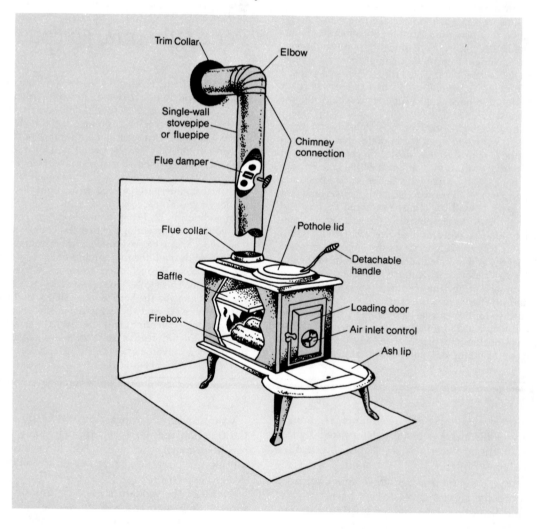

Anatomy of a Stove

Trim Collar

Elbow

Single-wall stovepipe or fluepipe

Chimney connection

Flue damper

Flue collar

Pothole lid

Detachable handle

Baffle

Firebox

Loading door

Air inlet control

Ash lip

How they work

Unlike fireplaces, wood stoves work on the principle of controlled combustion. In a fireplace there is no way to restrict the amount of air feeding the fire, so it burns uncontrolled and uses large amounts of wood. Most of the heat produced by the fire escapes up the chimney.

In a stove, the burning rate is controlled by either adjustable air inlets on the stove itself or by a damper in the flue pipe, or both. Airtight stoves are more efficient than nonairtight ones, because in a non-airtight stove excess air can leak through cracks and crevices to lower combustion efficiency. Airtight stoves are designed to introduce the right amount of air precisely where it's needed for most efficient combustion.

A truly efficient stove is also designed to burn a greater percentage of volatile gases produced by burning wood (discussed on page 8). To do this, the airflow pattern (draft) in the stove must restrict these gases and reroute them over the flame or into a secondary combustion area within the stove where the temperature is high enough to ignite the gases.

Draft and stove design. The stove's design determines the airflow pattern set up when the stove is operating. The drawings below show the standard "draft" designs of stoves. The draft patterns themselves do not determine the stove's ability to burn the volatile gases, so one can't be recommended over another. Efficient secondary combustion depends on the way the stove is designed to take advantage of its draft pattern, such as where secondary combustion takes place, location of secondary air inlets, size and shape of firebox, and other considerations.

How they heat

Heat travels in three ways: conduction, radiation, and convection.

When a fire is built in a stove, heat is conducted through the stove body—*conduction* is the movement of heat through a solid material from a hotter to a colder surface.

When the metal stove body heats up, the heat is radiated into the room. *Radiation* is the direct transmission of energy in the form of infrared rays; these

Stove Draft Designs

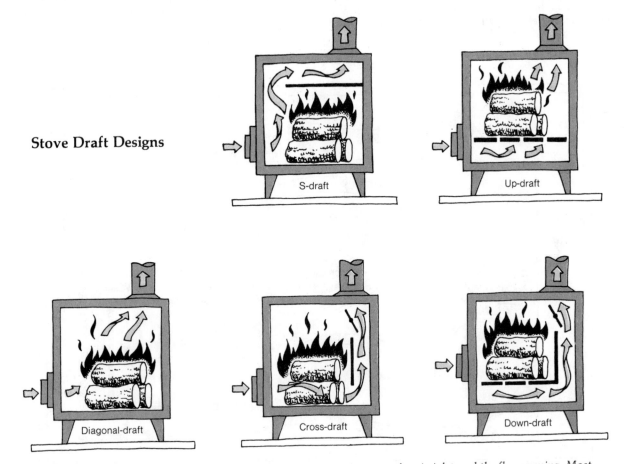

Draft pattern *refers to the course air takes through the stove between the air inlet and the flue opening. Most stoves use one of the five draft patterns shown here, or a variation of these. As illustrated, the internal design of the stove (location of air inlets, grates, baffles, etc.) determines its draft pattern.*

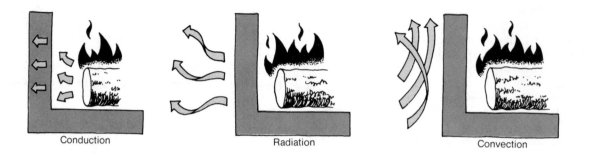

Conduction   Radiation   Convection

rays will heat objects they strike, though they don't contribute to heating the air space in between. Wood stoves heat primarily by radiation.

Convection is the movement of heat through air or fluids. When air is heated, it rises, setting up convective currents. Some stoves, called circulating stoves or heaters, have an outer metal jacket surrounding the firebox, with a 2-inch to 6-inch airspace in between. As the stove heats up this airspace, cold room air is drawn through vents near the bottom, heated, and expelled through the top (see drawing below). With some stoves, a fan is used to speed up this process, making the stove more efficient (similar to a forced air furnace).

The basic principles of stove operation discussed here apply to most stoves on the market today. Explanations on how individual stoves work (provided by the stove dealer or in manufacturer's literature) may tend to be more technical and complicated, and you may want to ask about them. But remember that the most important thing is not *how* a stove works, but *how well* it works. For information on choosing a stove for your heating needs, see pages 19–22.

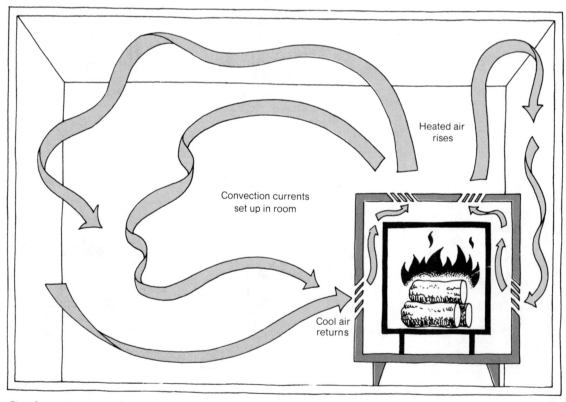

Heated air rises

Convection currents set up in room

Cool air returns

Circulating stoves *work by convection. Arrows show how heated air rises from the stove, is cooled, and returns to the stove through vents near its bottom.*

Wood stoves & the solar home

If you own or are planning a solar home, you have probably run into the problem of back-up heating. In most areas of the country, codes require that you install a back-up system capable of heating your home on days when the solar system is not operating. Until recently, this usually meant a full-fledged central heating system. The expense of such a system can be considerable and may discourage you from even attempting solar heating—especially if the solar design is efficient and the back-up system will not see much use. Wood stoves can be the answer to this dilemma.

Many areas now accept wood stoves as the sole source of heat in a home; and, as reliable methods of rating a stove's output evolve, the trend is likely to spread. This opens the door to the use of wood stoves as efficient, inexpensive auxiliary heaters in solar construction.

Wood/solar compatibility

Solar homes and wood stoves are uniquely compatible. Many solar structures have large amounts of brick, tile, concrete, or other heavy material built into their walls and floors. This is called "thermal mass" and is used as a means of storing the sun's radiant energy. The thermal mass will also store radiant energy from a wood stove, and this will tend to equalize the rise and fall of the stove's heat output as the wood is alternately added and allowed to burn down to coals.

In addition, a solar home's open-space planning—designed to promote circulation of heat—is ideal for a centrally located radiant heater, such as a wood stove. The relative lack of full-height interior walls readily allows for natural convection throughout the house, while any area from which you can see the stove will receive direct, radiant heat.

You can also tie your wood stove into the solar system itself, using the stove to boost the system's output on cloudy or especially cold days (see drawings). In this arrangement, the stove does double duty: as an independent space heater and as an active link in the solar heating system. But be sure to consult an experienced solar designer before attempting any such installation.

The future is now

As fossil fuel supplies continue to dwindle, the nation's forests and the sun are increasingly becoming practical alternate sources of energy, especially for the homeowner. The future looks bright for both wood and solar heating; for examples of how some homeowners have combined the two, see pages 44, 46, 48, 55, and 62.

Water-filled columns *of this passive solar heating system store heat from both the sun and the stove.*

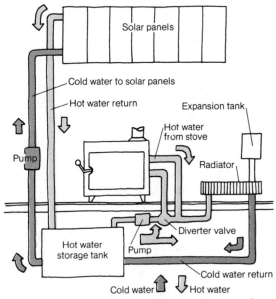

Active system *allows either solar panels or wood stove to become the primary heat source.*

Determining Your Heating Needs

Whether you plan to heat your entire home with wood, or just part of it, you must determine how much heat is needed, then select a stove to fill your heating requirements. This would be a simple matter if you only had to determine how much heat your present system delivers to the area you want heated, then install one or two stoves that provide that amount of heat. Unfortunately, there are several factors that make this more complicated:

1. Because stoves are primarily radiant heaters, they'll usually heat the room they're in and a few surrounding rooms if there are no obstructions such as walls or partitions to block the radiant heat. In order to heat outlying rooms, you must either find a way to transfer the stove's heat to them or install additional stoves.

2. It's difficult to calculate how much heat a stove delivers. The heat output of a stove will vary depending on the amount and type of wood used for each firing and how the stove is operated during that time. The location of the stove, length of inside flue pipe, and height and location of outside chimney also affect the stove's heat output. This does not take into account the stove design and its initial heat output.

3. The stove industry has not yet established accurate standards for rating the average heat output of stoves on the market. Many stove manufacturers attempt to rate their stoves by testing them under controlled conditions, but they cannot take into account your individual requirements for heating your home or the way you will use your stove.

The revival of the wood stove industry, with its continuing development of more efficient heating devices, is still young. In time, manufacturers will undoubtedly develop more standardized methods of rating heat output and heating efficiency. For now,

the best way to choose the right stove for your heating needs is to rely on the experience of reputable stove dealers and installers who are familiar with your geographical area and the capabilities of their products.

In order for a stove dealer or installer to be most helpful, though, you should be able to clearly define your heating requirements and provide accurate information regarding the area you wish to heat.

Defining your needs

First, you must decide whether wood will be the primary source of heat or whether you'll be using the wood stove for supplemental heat. Unless you've had prior experience with wood stoves and are thoroughly familiar with them, your best bet is to start with one stove to supplement your present heating system. This way you can find out if wood-burning is generally compatible with your life style.

If you're planning a new home with wood as the primary source of heat, you should plan to have a back-up heating system. Some new homes are designed to integrate wood stoves with active or passive solar heating systems. If this appeals to you, find a local architect who can advise you on the practicality of these systems in your area. (See "Wood stoves & the solar home," page 13.)

Area to be heated

First, how much living space do you want to heat? If you plan to take a big load off your present heating system, the best location for the stove is in the main living area. The living room, or perhaps family room, is usually the largest room in the house; it is often centrally located, making it easier to transfer heat to surrounding rooms. If the living space you want to heat is spread out, separated by walls or intervening rooms, you'll need a way to duct the heat from the "stove room" to those rooms.

Once you've decided which rooms you'll be heating, you'll need to provide the stove dealer with the following information:

A basic floor plan. If you're going to be heating more than one room, make a rough floor plan of the living space to be heated, indicating sizes of rooms and locations of openings (doors, windows), dividers, and partitions. If you own a two-story home and plan to heat upstairs rooms, include an elevation drawing indicating rooms and location of stairwell. Be sure to include the pitch and overall height of the roof to determine the amount of flue pipe required.

Cubic feet of living space to be heated. To find the cubic feet of each room to be heated, first find the square feet of floor space (length of room times width), then multiply this figure by the ceiling height. If the room is irregularly shaped, such as an "L" shaped room, divide the area into squares or rectangles, find the square feet of each, then add them to get the total.

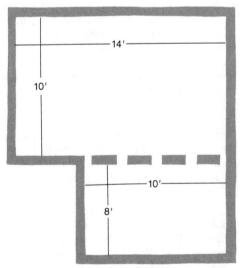

Cubic feet *in L-shaped room: (10' x 8') + (10' x 14') = 220 sq. ft. Multiply by ceiling height (8') to get 1760 cubic feet.*

Heat loss factors. If you don't already know, find out if the walls and ceilings are insulated. In houses with unfinished attics, the ceiling insulation will be between the joists of the attic floor. Note down the type of insulation and its "R" value (usually printed on blanket-type insulation). If you can't find the "R" value, measure the thickness of the insulation. To

check for insulation in exterior walls and ceilings where joists are not visible from the attic, turn off the power and remove a switch or receptacle cover and a ceiling fixture. You should then be able to see if there's insulation between the wall studs and ceiling joists.

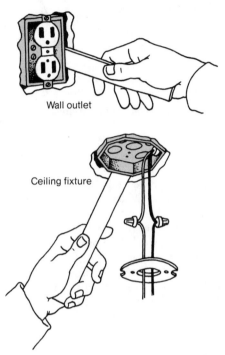

Wall outlet

Ceiling fixture

To find insulation, *remove wall outlet cover. Check for insulation around ceiling fixture.*

Also note the number and size of windows and whether or not windows and doors are weather-stripped. If you don't have insulation or weather-stripping and you're serious about reducing heating costs, plan to add these *before* you install your stove. A well-insulated house requires less heat and consequently a smaller stove. For more information on the subject, refer to the *Sunset* book *Do-It-Yourself Insulation & Weatherstripping.*

Where to put the stove

Once you've determined the living space you'll be heating, you will have to decide which room should have the stove and where the stove should go in the room. This is an important decision because the stove's location will determine how well the stove heats the living space; once it's installed, the stove, its hearth, and flue system are not easily moved.

Which room? Ideally, the stove should be located as near the center of the house as possible so its heat will be evenly distributed throughout the main living area. In most houses, this location is likely to be the

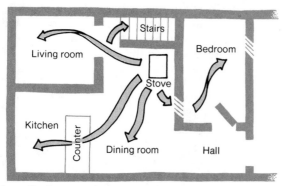

Centrally locating *the stove in the house will enable it to heat more living space.*

family room or living room, also the spot where family members spend most of their leisure time and where family activities take place.

Of course, your heating needs may not coincide with this idea. You may need a small stove in the bedroom that's "never quite warm enough" at night, or in a detached workshop or other room not heated by your present system.

In two-story houses, placing the stove near the stairwell will help heat the upstairs rooms. Or you can install floor registers to heat the room directly above the one with the stove.

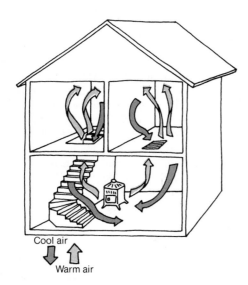

To help heat upstairs, *place stove near stairwell; install floor vents to allow heat to rise naturally.*

Because heat rises, it would seem logical to put the stove in the basement if you have one, and install floor vents or registers on the first floor to let the heat through. But with wood stoves and other radiant-type heaters, this practice is often inefficient, because much of the stove's heat is absorbed by the basement walls, especially if they're not insulated. But if you're installing a woodburning furnace that transfers its heat by means of fans and/or ductwork, the basement is the logical place to put it (see "Wood furnaces," page 89).

If you plan to install vents or registers in the wall or floor to transfer the stove's heat to other rooms, you should first check with your building department. Most local building departments have code requirements on the types of vents used and their locations in the house. Your building department can advise you on these requirements, as well as those for air ducting and other heat transfer systems.

It's also a good idea to use vents that have adjustable louvers, so the vents can be closed when not in use. These vents allow you to adjust the amount of heat entering rooms—and when closed, they also shut off noises coming from adjacent rooms. You can buy them from furnace or heating suppliers.

If one room in your house is lower than the rest (such as a sunken living room or conversation pit) that room will probably be a bit cooler than the others. A stove in this location helps compensate for the fact that hot air rises and cool air settles at the lowest spot in the house. In addition to heating the cool room, the stove's heat will also circulate more efficiently to other parts of the house.

If the thermostat for your present heating system is in the room where you want your stove to be, you'll have to relocate the thermostat or adjust it to compensate for the stove's heat.

Placement within a room. You will want to put your stove where it fits comfortably into your room decor —after all, the stove and its hearth, like a piece of furniture, will be an integral part of your room's interior design. It should, like other household appliances, be placed where it's convenient to use. But a stove's placement will be limited to where you can run the flue pipe and install the chimney (see "Chimney installation," page 71).

When deciding where your stove will go, you'll have to take into account required clearances from combustible surfaces and materials—walls, furniture, wood floors, etc. (See "Stove & stovepipe clearances," page 67.) Also consider the type of hearth you want and choose the best spot for it.

The stove's location in the room will also have an effect on its heating efficiency. If you put a radiant stove near a picture window or outside wall, some of its radiant heat will be lost to the outside. On the other hand, placing the stove in the center of the room will take advantage of the full radiation pattern.

Stoves can be vented into existing chimneys or fireplaces to save the additional expense of installing

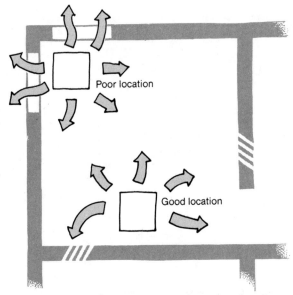

Good stove location *in room takes advantage of optimum radiant heat transmission of stove.*

a separate chimney. Several examples appear on pages 60 and 61. To do this, you'll have to have the chimney inspected to make sure it's safe, and completely block off the fireplace opening except where the flue pipe enters. For details on how to do this, see "Venting into the fireplace," page 76.

Desired temperature

People are different, and so are their temperature requirements. Some people are perfectly comfortable in

a room at 68°F/20°C; others put on their sweaters when the temperature drops below 70°F/21°C.

Most of us are used to fossil fuel or electric heating, whereby every room in the house is heated, more or less, to a consistent temperature. Because the heat output of a stove fluctuates during the burning process, so will the room temperature. Some stoves —such as those with automatic thermostats—provide a more consistent heat than others, though, so keep this in mind when shopping for one. And you will have to become accustomed to these variations in temperature and learn how to operate your stove to keep them to a minimum.

Even if your entire home were heated with wood stoves, it would be difficult to keep every room the same temperature. The rooms farthest from the stove would always be a little cooler. Often, those who heat with wood find there is no need to heat unused rooms, and they plan their family activities in the room with the stove. And you may change your habits slightly; maybe you'll close doors to rooms that are not in use and heat them only when necessary. You might want to throw a few extra blankets on the bed, because the fire will die down at night, or you can rely on your present heating system to make up the difference.

When discussing your heating needs with the stove dealer, be sure to include your temperature requirements. What is a comfortable temperature for you? How many rooms do you want heated to this temperature, and at what hours of the day?

A word of caution: In very cold climates, you'll have to keep all rooms with plumbing warm enough to prevent water pipes from freezing.

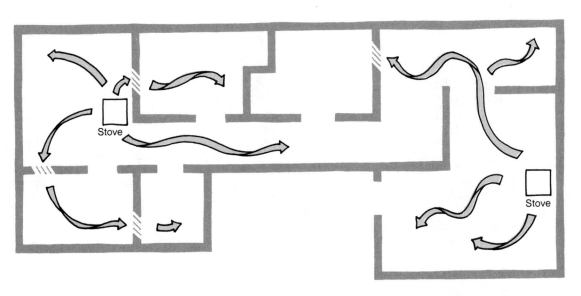

If your floorplan *is spread out like this one, you may need another stove to heat outlying rooms, or at least a method of transferring one stove's heat to all rooms.*

Wood stoves for mobile homes

If you have a mobile home, a wood stove may be the answer to high bills for electric and bottled gas heat, and there are several wood stoves on the market designed specifically for mobile homes. Some are simple in appearance, and others are elaborate, with fire-view doors, ovens, thermostats, and circulating air jackets.

Only a stove specifically designed for mobile home installation should be considered. A conventional wood stove might be unsafe and would certainly be illegal.

Mobile home stoves must meet stringent Department of Housing and Urban Development (HUD) standards. These standards require that the stove draw its combustion air from outside the dwelling, that the chimney be made of insulated Class-A pipe (no single-wall pipe may be used), and that the hearth meet certain minimum dimensions. You must fasten the stove down, and your chimney must be demountable for transport. In addition, you may not install the stove in a room used for sleeping.

Each HUD-approved stove will have its own standards for clearance from combustible walls and floors. Some stoves allow "zero clearance" and can be set right against the wall and floor—certainly an advantage where space is at a premium.

When shopping for a mobile home stove, be sure to check that it has been tested and approved for mobile home use by a federally certified testing laboratory— only such stoves may be installed in mobile homes. Then follow the manufacturer's directions carefully when installing your stove; this will assure your compliance with HUD requirements. Check local codes as well, however; they may be even stricter than the federal standards.

If you can meet these requirements, a wood stove may be an ideal solution to the problem of heating your mobile home. Remember, however, that seasoned hardwood weighs up to 4,000 pounds per cord. At that weight, you won't want to be taking it with you, so you might want to stay in one place during the heating season.

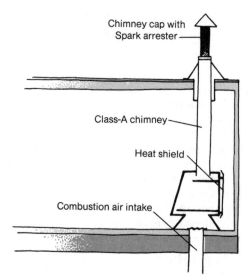

Wood stoves *intended for mobile homes must be especially designed to meet HUD standards above. These stoves can provide significant economy over conventional heating.*

Styles vary: *Mobile-home stoves range from the simple to the complex. Each stove shown above meets HUD standards. Stove at left is a simple radiant heater with rear shield; middle stove adds thermostatic draft control, fireview door. Stove at right has similar features plus an oven, and allows zero-clearance installation.*

Finding a Stove That Fills Your Needs

Your first priority will be to choose a stove that will adequately heat your living space. The key requirement here is the stove's *heating capacity*, or the maximum amount of heat a stove can deliver over a given period of time when operated at the upper end of its heat output range.

Second, choose a stove that will provide the maximum amount of heat possible from each cord of wood. The heat output in relation to the amount of wood burned is referred to as the stove's *heating efficiency.*

Finally, you should have control over the stove's heat output in order to maintain an even room temperature in your home. The stove should deliver an even, consistent heat over a long period of time so you won't be constantly refueling it and continually adjusting the damper controls.

Heating capacity

Wood stoves can provide a wide range of heat outputs, depending on how much wood is fed into them and how much air is provided for combustion. When the stove is delivering the maximum amount of heat possible under safe operating conditions, the amount of heat delivered is its heating capacity.

The heating capacity of fossil-fueled and electric heaters is measured in BTUs per hour (one BTU or British Thermal Unit is the amount of heat required to raise the temperature of one pound of water by 1°F). Because these appliances produce an even, consistent heat when operated at their maximum heat output, it's relatively easy to give them BTU ratings.

The maximum heat output of a wood stove is somewhat more difficult to establish—different types of wood and their moisture content affect a stove's

heat output; so does the amount of wood and what stage of the burning process it's going through. Even if the stove is operating at maximum capacity, the heat output fluctuates over a period of an hour, so BTU ratings for wood stoves are usually no more than estimates. Many stove manufacturers attempt to give their stoves BTU ratings, but their estimates vary in accuracy, depending on how they test their stoves. Manufacturers' ratings do, however, give you a rough idea of a stove's heating capacity, and they indicate which stoves throw off more heat. The heating capacities of stoves vary considerably—from less than 10,000 to well over 100,000 BTUs per hour.

At present, the stove industry as a whole is in the process of standardizing testing methods to determine the heating capacity of stoves. This will provide the consumer with more accurate information on the heating capacities of the various stoves on the market. But until set standards and formulas are developed for matching stoves to individual heating needs, you must rely on the experience of stove dealers, installers, and users. People in your area who've installed stoves in houses similar to yours are a good source of information.

Matching the stove to your living space

It's important that the heating capacity of the stove you choose matches your heating requirements as closely as possible. If the stove is oversized, it will constantly have to be damped down (operated at a low heat output) so it won't overheat the room. This causes the fire to smolder, which lowers the stove's heating efficiency and causes excess creosote to build up in the flue pipe. Of course, an undersized stove won't adequately heat the room, or it will have to be overfired to do so—making it unsafe and shortening its useful life. You should choose a stove that has a slightly higher heating capacity than the living space requires, so that you'll be operating it just below its maximum heat output level. Generally, stoves are most efficient when they operate at 75 percent of their maximum capacity.

The physical size of the stove doesn't always determine how much heat it throws off. A small, heat-efficient, airtight stove may have the same heating capacity as a large, drafty Franklin, but use only half as much wood. Generally speaking, though, of two different size stoves with equal heating efficiencies, the larger stove will have the higher heating capacity.

A stove's heating capacity should not be confused with its fuel capacity (the amount of wood that can be loaded into the firebox). Both fuel capacity and heating efficiency determine heating capacity, so the larger stove is not always the better buy.

Some manufacturers rate the heating capacity of their stoves according to how many cubic feet (or even square feet) of living space the stove will heat. Their figures may seem helpful in matching a stove to your living space, but the figures are subject to interpretation—they don't take into account differences in climates, houses, amount and kind of wood burned, and other variables governing heat output discussed previously.

Heating efficiency

A stove's heating efficiency is based on the percentage of wood's potential (stored) heat the stove is able to convert to useful heat. This depends on how efficiently the stove burns the wood (combustion efficiency) and how much of that heat is transferred into the room (heat transfer efficiency).

Efficiency ratings

Modern airtight stoves are anywhere from 40 to 60 percent efficient; conventional masonry fireplaces, for comparison, are 10 percent efficient, or less. (In a fireplace, 90 percent of the fire's heat escapes up the chimney along with the smoke.) Nonairtight stoves, which include Franklin stoves and antique stoves and their reproductions, are about 30 percent efficient.

Some manufacturers give their stoves efficiency ratings, though their figures are usually just estimates based on specific test cases. The stove you buy, once it's installed in your home, may be more or less efficient than the manufacturer's claims, but their figures may serve as a general comparison.

The heating efficiency of any stove will be affected by its location, flue pipe, and chimney installation, and by the way you operate the stove. But some stoves are inherently more efficient than others; and that efficiency is determined by the stove's design, the materials used in its construction, and the quality of workmanship that goes into its manufacture. Un-

less you have access to an unlimited wood supply and don't mind cutting and storing it, you'll probably want the most heat-efficient stove you can afford, provided it satisfies your other requirements.

Combustion

The combustion efficiency of a stove relates to how completely the stove burns wood to render as much of the wood's potential heat as possible. How stoves accomplish this is discussed in "How they work," page 11. How efficiently they accomplish it is another question.

Airtightness. Part of a stove's combustion efficiency depends on its airtightness. The so-called airtight stoves are not literally airtight — they're not able to hold air under pressure, or even water, for that matter. A good airtight stove, though, is sealed well enough so that the air necessary for combustion enters only through the air inlets. Any minute quantities of air that may leak through doors or movable parts will not affect combustion efficiency.

Steel stoves are made airtight by welding the seams or joints between the steel plates; the joints in cast-iron stoves are bolted together and sealed with furnace cement.

Before you buy any stove, check all seams and joints carefully for possible air leaks. A flashlight is helpful here—if the joints leak light, they will also leak air. Also check cast iron stoves for cracks and poorly fitted castings. The most common culprit in a leaky stove, though, is a poor seal or fit of the loading door. Inspect the door's gasket and check to see if the door fits snugly against the stove body.

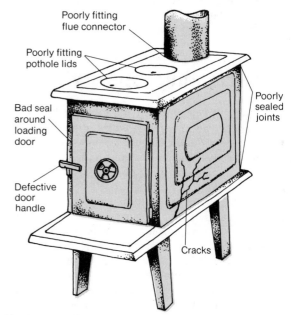

Poorly fitting flue connector

Poorly fitting pothole lids

Bad seal around loading door

Defective door handle

Poorly sealed joints

Cracks

Check stove *carefully for leaks before you buy it; using a flashlight inside will help.*

Heat-recovery devices

Some stoves and freestanding fireplaces waste heat. Either they operate with too hot a flue-gas temperature or their heat transfer efficiency is poor. (See pages 11 and 22 for a discussion of these concepts.) Heat-recovery devices are designed to reclaim some of this wasted heat.

Most of these heat-recovery devices fall into one of two categories: passive or active. The passive devices add extra surface area to the stove or flue pipe to increase the output of radiant heat. This increase in radiant surface area also increases air convection past the stove's warm surfaces (see page 12 for a discussion of radiation and convection). Active devices use a fan, blower, or pump to force air or water through the system. A simple passive device might do the job. If not, consider going a step further with an active device. But don't go either route unless you fully understand the possible results and consequences (see "A few cautions," below right).

Passive heat recovery

A stove's heat output partly depends on its capability to radiate the fire's heat. If a stove sends too much of its heat up the flue, then increasing the radiant surface area of the stove or flue will increase the efficiency of the unit.

You can accomplish this by placing the stove where it will have a long run of single-wall pipe in the room, or by adding accessory fins and radiators to the pipe itself (see drawing below). Flue pipe ovens and shelves also increase radiant surface area, and they have a further advantage of being very useful.

Some stoves have open-end pipes or tubes running through their fireboxes from bottom to top. Air is drawn into the bottom of the tubes and rises by convection out the top, thus heating the room and improving circulation of heat (see drawing below).

Active heat recovery

A fan above your stove will provide a simple form of active heat recovery. The fan moves down the heated air that naturally pools near the ceiling (see page 11), and promotes circulation of warm air to all corners of the room.

A more complicated form of active heat recovery is a powered heat exchanger. You might consider adding one to your flue pipe installation (see drawing below).

Powered heat exchangers are best suited to units that tend to have high flue-gas temperatures, such as freestanding fireplaces or Franklin stoves. They should *not* be used with efficient, airtight stoves because they will cool the flue too much and set up a chain reaction: loss of draft, damping of the fire, and excessive creosote buildup in the flue that can cause a chimney fire.

Some stoves offer powered systems that force air over the surface of the stove itself or through pipes contained in the firebox. Other stoves heat water in firebox pipe systems. The heated water can be pumped to radiators and hot water heaters in other rooms, and can also be used to preheat the cold air return of a central heating system.

A few cautions

Remember that the concept of heat recovery is subject to the law of diminishing returns. Robbing the flue pipe of too much heat can lower its temperature to the point where excess creosote will form—creating the danger of a chimney fire, or at least the need for more frequent flue cleaning. Taking out too much heat may also retard the stove's draft.

Consider cost, as well; many add-on devices are expensive. In some cases, the return in reclaimed heat may not justify the cost of its recovery.

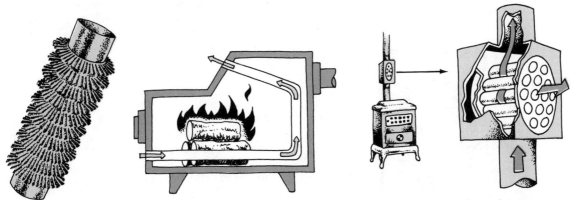

Simple add-on fins (*left*) *greatly increase the flue pipe's radiant area. Fire-box pipe system* (*center*) *increases natural convection, can take a blower. Fan-powered heat exchanger* (*right*) *extracts heat from flue gases flowing around its battery of air pipes.*

Stove design. The design elements of a stove—such as location of air inlets, the draft pattern employed, where secondary combustion takes place, and the stove's ability to maintain the proper firebox temperature—will initially determine its combustion efficiency. All of these factors work together in a good stove design. There is no right or wrong way to design a stove, other than utilizing the basic principles discussed in "How they work," page 11. Because one design of Scandinavian or downdraft stove is efficient, it doesn't necessarily follow that another one will be, even if it is virtually the same in size and appearance. To find out which stove designs are most efficient, ask dealers for performance data and get at least two opinions on each brand you're considering.

Heat transfer

The heat generated inside the stove is transferred into the room by first conducting through the stove walls, then radiating from their surfaces. How well a stove transfers heat—its heat transfer efficiency—depends on three factors: 1) the amount of surface area radiating heat in relationship to the overall size of the stove; 2) the ability of the stove material to conduct heat; 3) the stove's ability to keep hot flue gases in contact with the inside walls of the firebox. An efficient stove transfers the maximum amount of heat possible while retaining high enough firebox temperatures to support efficient combustion.

Several methods are used in stove design to increase a stove's radiating surface without increasing the size of the firebox. Some stoves have a secondary chamber above the firebox to extract more heat from flue gases before they go up the chimney. On other stoves, the sides of the firebox are heavily embossed with patterns or designs that add more radiating surface to the firebox.

Heat is also transferred through the walls of the flue pipe. A long flue pipe inside the room will radiate more heat than a short one, but if a flue

pipe radiates too much heat, the rising flue gases will cool off too quickly and the chimney won't draw properly. This also causes excess creosote buildup in the flue pipe. For more information see "Chimney installation," page 71. You can improve the flue pipe's heat transfer efficiency by adding a heat recovery device to increase the pipe's radiant surface (see page 21).

To keep hot gases in contact with the stove walls, the stove's draft pattern must keep the gases moving by creating turbulence inside the firebox.

Some materials transfer heat better than others; both cast iron and steel conduct and radiate heat very well. The gauge of metal used in a stove does not significantly affect its heat transfer efficiency. Thin-walled stoves transfer heat quickly—they heat up fast and cool off fast. Thick-walled stoves will transfer the same amount of heat, only more slowly over a longer period of time. Both have their advantages and disadvantages, as discussed in "Choosing a durable stove," page 26.

Keeping an even heat

In order to keep an even, consistent room temperature, you must be able to control the stove's heat output. On most stoves, this requires adjusting the air inlets or damper controls to control the burning rate of the fire. Some stoves allow more control over the burning rate than others, so they can provide a wider range of heat outputs. Control over the burning rate also enables the stove to hold a fire longer. Many of the modern airtight stoves will hold a fire overnight when operated at a low heat output. The thickness of the metal in the stove has an effect on the steadiness of heat output. As mentioned, a thin-walled stove heats up fast and cools off fast; it's also more sensitive to the fluctuations in heat produced by the fire. Thick-walled stoves tend to have a more even heat output because some of the fire's heat is stored in the stove body and released more gradually.

Generally, a larger, heavier stove with an efficient damper control and a large fuel capacity (amount of wood that will fit in the firebox) delivers a steadier, more even heat because its mass is greater and it doesn't have to be refueled as often.

Thermostats. On most stoves, the air inlets or damper controls are manually operated. In order to maintain an even room temperature, they must be adjusted periodically. On some stoves the air inlets are thermostatically controlled. The thermostats automatically adjust the air inlets and, therefore, the amount of combustion air entering the stove. You can set the thermostat to a predetermined temperature range, just as you would with other heating devices, and eliminate the need to keep an eye on the stove's heat output.

Secondary chamber *increases radiating surface of stove to improve heat transfer from fire.*

Buying a Stove

Having worked out your heating requirements, you're ready to select a stove. Your range of choices is now limited to those that will meet your particular heating needs. From these, you'll want to choose a stove that's attractive, durable, and convenient to use. You might also want such options as a large cooking surface, water heating capability, or an enamel finish other than the traditional black. Today's wood stove market offers a wide variety, so try to see as many stoves as you can before making your final decision.

You should talk to stove owners who are experienced in heating with wood, as well as the stove dealers you visit. The information on the following pages will help you recognize a quality stove, though no comparison of specific brands is made.

Check on insurance. Before you actually buy your stove and the necessary components for its installation and use, check with your insurance company. Most companies require that you inform them of any major changes or additions to your home that may affect safety.

If you already have fire insurance, you'll probably not need any additional insurance when you install a wood stove. However, the insurance company will probably require that the stove and its installation meet certain fire safety requirements in order for your present policy to cover any fire damage caused by the stove or chimney installation. Some companies may refuse to pay for damage in the event of a fire that can be traced directly to an unsafe stove installation.

A word on price. You'll be better off in the long run if you buy the best stove you can afford. Price doesn't necessarily determine a stove's quality, but the more efficient, durable stoves do usually cost more than their poorly built, inefficient counterparts. Most likely, the extra money you spend on a good stove will be returned to you in savings on wood over a few seasons—and a well-built stove will last longer. You'll probably be paying at least several hundred dollars for the chimney installation and at least another hundred for the hearth, so it makes sense to buy a quality stove that will give many years of good service.

Know what you're buying

Even the most durable stove will not last indefinitely, so it's important that both stove manufacturer and dealer stand behind their product. You should be assured that you're getting everything you've paid for and, even more important, that if you encounter any difficulties with the stove after you've bought it, they can be easily corrected.

Stove dealers

Throughout the past two chapters, reference has been made to working with reputable and experienced stove dealers. A reputable stove dealer is simply one with a proven track record. The dealer should be able to help you determine your needs, answer your questions honestly, and be willing to visit your home to get a first-hand look at your situation. You're better off working with a dealer who is an established member of your community and familiar with your area. A good dealer will be able to provide you with names

(Continued on page 26)

Buying & restoring an antique stove

Antique stoves have a unique appeal that many modern stoves can't match. Shopping for and fixing up an old stove can be an adventure in itself—an adventure that can be stimulating or fraught with headaches. Here are some pointers.

Shopping for a stove

Knowing where to look and what to look for is at least half the battle. You might be lucky; there might be a dealer in your area who specializes in antique stoves and who is no farther away than your phone book. But it is far more likely that you'll have to put in time making the rounds of antique stores, junk shops, and auctions before you find the stove that's right for you.

Once you've found a likely candidate, you'll need to examine it for damage, especially if it's quite old and you plan to use it regularly.

Most older stoves that have survived are made of cast iron and may be cracked and rusted. Carefully examine the corners and firebox for cracks—a flashlight will help here, and it's always wise to carry one with you when you're shopping for a vintage stove. Check the stove top for damage, and see that the dampers and draft controls are working. Inspect plated parts, if any; replating is one of the most expensive jobs in a stove restoration project.

Restoring an antique stove

Don't automatically abandon your project if you find some damage. Many repairs are easily accomplished; others may be more involved but still within the realm of feasibility. For help of various kinds, check the Yellow Pages under "Foundries," "Plating," and "Welding."

Simple repairs. Cracks can be mended by a qualified welder. For iron stoves, cast-iron rod and flux are used. If the crack is longer than about 3 inches, the stove should be disassembled and the cracked piece pre-heated to a dull red before welding; this will equalize heat stress. The part should be covered and allowed to cool slowly after the job is done.

Recasting. Badly damaged pieces can often be recast at local foundries if you supply a form from which a sand mold can be made. To do this, repair the broken part with automobile body compound, finishing it as carefully as possible; the new part will exactly duplicate your repaired original.

Large parts can also be recast, but you need to take shrinkage into account here; castings shrink about 1/8 inch per foot as they cool, and while this is not a problem with small pieces, larger ones may not fit after

they are finished. In such cases it might be possible to make a slightly larger wooden model of the piece you want and have the foundry work from that. Shop for prices—many foundries charge by the pound, and rates vary.

Replating ornamental parts. Prices vary considerably for this job, too. Most of the cost of replating goes into the labor needed for surface preparation, and you get what you pay for. Some shops have been known to plate right over the pitting that rust leaves, so look for a shop that has a reputation for doing high-quality work.

Finding replacement parts. Sometimes it's possible to find original parts for an old stove. If you select a brand known to have been popular in its day, or if it was made by a foundry that is still in business, the chances of finding spare parts are greatly improved. A little research before buying will help you here.

Refinishing your antique. Once your stove is in good working order, you'll want to give some thought to its final appearance. Part of the charm of an antique is tangible evidence of age. You probably don't want your stove to be covered with rust; on the other hand, if you go after every speck of rust, your stove is likely to appear either brand-new or seriously abraded.

Avoid the use of sandpaper, wire brushes, and sandblasting. Try a jelly-type rust remover instead. Once the surface is clean, use stove polish or a light coat of high-heat paint to finish off the job.

Living with your antique stove

Now it is time to make the stove a part of your home. Though installation, use, and maintenance of an antique stove come under the same standards and principles as modern wood stoves, there are some additional considerations.

Installation. Even a simple antique stove tends to become a focal point in a room, and a truly elaborate one can be strikingly dominant. Careful attention to hearth placement and design is therefore even more important than usual.

Use and maintenance. Your antique stove can be an "old gentleman" or simply a curmudgeon; the difference lies in how it is used and maintained. Bear in mind that the stove has already had a long life of service. It is not new. Exercise restraint in firing the stove, and keep a careful eye on it for mechanical problems. Gently treated, it's likely to warm you for years to come.

Old standby, *the potbelly stove once warmed
trainmen in cabooses, passengers in stations, and
whittlers relaxing in the general store. When added to
your home, these stoves are uniquely evocative of a
bygone era.*

Basic box stove, *then as now, was the simplest wood-
burner. Old ones range from plain to ornate, can be
the most economical type for restoration. Small size
allows a wide range of applications.*

Ornate parlor stove *features extensive nickel plating,
Victorian filigree, and an urn for scented water.
Restoration can be quite a project, but one with
substantial rewards.*

Nineteenth-century range, *with its commanding
presence, will dominate any setting. It is truly the
ultimate in elaborate surface relief work—only the
functional cooktop has escaped embellishment.*

... *Continued from page 23*

of satisifed customers and the assurance that you'll be able to obtain both replacement parts and repair service should you need them in the future.

Some dealers employ their own installers. They'll be able to quote you a complete price that includes the cost of the stove as well as installation of the stove, chimney, and hearth. Others can recommend a reliable installer, or will help you do your own installation.

The revival of the wood stove industry has seen a number of new dealerships spring up across the country. They can offer you a high-quality product, but you would do well to question them carefully and try to determine if they'll still be around in several years should you need parts or service. Any able salesperson can give you a convincing sales pitch on the superiority of a product, but a reputable stove dealer will discuss both the strong points and the limitations of the stoves he has to offer.

Availability of parts

A well-built stove should last many years before parts need replacing. Occasionally, though, a part may break or wear out before its time. If this happens, the part should be readily available from the stove dealer or manufacturer. Grates, steel liners, and baffles, on the other hand, must be replaced periodically, so you want to be sure you can replace the parts you need.

The first question to ask yourself is: how long has the stove manufacturer been in business? The number of new stove manufacturers has increased greatly in the past few years, and it is likely many of them will be out of business over the next few. A stove manufacturer that has been in business for the past 10 years will probably still be around 10 or 20 years from now—and that in itself offers some assurance that replacement parts will be available.

The next question to ask is: how *readily* available are the parts? Winter can get awfully cold if you have to wait two months for a replacement part. A good stove dealer can get parts for you when you need them. If he carries foreign brand stoves, he'll usually stock spare parts.

A few cast-iron stoves have plates that are machined and fitted by hand, so they're not interchangeable. Should such a stove become damaged, you will have to ship the whole thing back to the factory for repair and probably pay shipping costs—unless you can repair it yourself or have it done locally. On most stoves, though, the parts are interchangeable, and many stove dealers stock spare parts for their stoves.

Parts for older or antique stoves may be difficult, if not impossible, to find. Any replacements will probably have to be custom-made to fit the stove. There are ways to accomplish this—see "Buying & restoring an antique stove," page 24.

Guarantees. Many stove manufacturers guarantee their stoves to indicate their durability and overall quality. Read the stove guarantee or warranty carefully. For how long is the stove guaranteed? Which parts are covered under the warranty? Is the guarantee unconditional or does it just cover defects in parts or labor? Always read the fine print.

What does the price include?

The price your dealer quotes you for the stove should be complete. It should include any shipping and delivery costs and any stove "accessories" that are essential to its operation. Such necessary items may include grates, flue adapters, handles for pot hole lids, and more. Next, figure in optional accessories such as ash shovels and buckets.

Chimney and hearth materials. The cost of chimney and hearth materials depends on the type of installation required and is figured separately from the price of the stove. Most dealers carry flue pipe and other chimney components and will advise you on what you'll need if you plan to install the stove yourself. Otherwise, the price of materials is usually included in the installation costs. For more information on chimney and hearth materials, see pages 67 and 69.

Will the stove fit?

The size and shape of a stove, along with its required clearances, dictate the amount of space you'll need for installation. A tall circular stove like the potbelly takes up less room than a box stove with the same surface area. Some stoves, including circulating heaters (page 12), require less clearance from floors and walls than others (see "Stove & stove pipe clearances," page 67).

Measure the stove you want and find out its required clearances before you buy it. You may either have to sacrifice a bit more living space for the stove you want or settle for a more compact stove with the same heating capabilities. Remember, too, that the more space required for the stove, the larger the hearth—and its cost.

Choosing a durable stove

The durability of a stove depends on the materials and workmanship that go into it. Most stoves are made of either cast iron or steel, or a combination of the two. Both have their advantages and disadvantages, but keep in mind that the quality of a stove is not determined by the *type* of material used to manufacture it, but by the *thickness* and *quality* of the materials and how well the stove *parts* are manufactured and assembled.

Cast-iron stoves

In cast-iron stoves, each part of the firebox is cast separately; the parts are then bolted together and the joints sealed with furnace cement. The edges of the castings are usually flanged so the seams overlap for a tighter fit. Cast-iron stove parts are thicker than those on most steel stoves, so cast-iron stoves are usually much heavier.

Advantages. Cast iron has long been the traditional material for wood stoves because of its resistance to warping at high temperatures or burning out after repeated firings. Cast-iron stoves will hold heat longer than thinner steel stoves, but it does take them longer to warm up (see "Heating efficiency," page 20).

Those who are familiar with cast-iron pans and griddles know that cast iron makes an excellent cooking surface—a consideration if you want a stove that allows you to grill food directly on the stove top.

Disadvantages. Cast iron is a brittle material susceptible to cracking, especially if poorly cast. It will crack if it is subjected to sudden or extreme changes in temperature, or if it is struck sharply with a heavy object such as a log. Overfiring the cast-iron stove or decreasing the firebox temperature suddenly (by throwing a frozen log in a hot fire or dousing the fire with water) will weaken or crack the stove.

When you buy a cast-iron stove, it must first be seasoned or tempered to prevent it from cracking. You do this by building a half-dozen or more small to moderate fires in the stove before using it at full capacity.

Because cast-iron stoves are heavy (some weigh over 300 pounds), they're not easily moved. The weight of the stove is an important consideration if you plan to dismantle and store it during the summer months.

The furnace cement used to seal cast-iron stoves becomes brittle over a period of time and will fall out. This causes the stove to lose its airtightness, so plan to replace the furnace cement periodically if you are buying a cast-iron stove. You can buy furnace cement at most hardware stores or stove dealers.

What to look for. First, check the stove for airtightness (page 20). When you shop, it's helpful to carry a flashlight with you to inspect the stove's interior. Make sure the castings fit properly and are sealed adequately. Next, check to make sure there are no thin spots in the castings. Check all parts for cracks—sometimes cast-iron stoves get cracked in shipping. Look for pitted, porous, or rough surfaces—often a sign of poor castings. Generally you need only compare an expensive cast-iron stove with a cheap one

to recognize quality casting. Finally, check for missing parts and make sure all movable parts work properly.

Steel stoves

Steel stoves are made from sheet steel that varies in quality according to thickness. Steel thickness is measured by gauge number—the *smaller* the gauge number, the *thicker* the steel.

The pieces of a steel stove are cut out with a torch and welded together. Some steel stoves are built from several gauges of steel, with the thicker steel (12 gauge or thicker) used where it is necessary. (Refer to the chart on this page for comparative thicknesses of gauge numbers.) Other stoves are a combination of steel and cast iron—an attempt to provide the best qualities of both materials. Many steel stoves, for instance, have cast-iron doors to minimize warping around the door seal. The more expensive steel stoves are made from plate steel (3/16" or thicker) and are comparable to cast iron in durability. Stoves made from thin steel sheets are often referred to as sheet metal stoves, or sometimes called "tin" stoves because their predecessors were made from light-gauge tin. These lightweight stoves, weighing 75 pounds or less, are relatively inexpensive ($100 to $150) and are suitable for temporary or emergency heating. But, they are not durable and will burn out after one or two seasons of constant use. The life of these stoves can be extended by lining the inside with firebrick.

Approximate thicknesses of sheet metal gauge numbers in fractions of an inch.			
Gauge	Thickness	Gauge	Thickness
0	5/16	10	9/64
1	9/32	12	7/64
2	17/64	14	5/64
3	1/4	16	1/16
4	15/64	18	1/20
5	7/32	20	3/80
6	13/64	22	1/32
7	3/16	24	1/40
8	11/64	26	3/160
9	5/32	28	1/64

Advantages. The lighter gauge steel metal stoves have the advantage of being easily portable. You can use them for temporary supplemental heat or for emergencies such as power outages or fuel shortages. They also transfer heat more quickly than heavier stoves, and thus can heat a room in just a few minutes.

Heavier gauge steel stoves have much the same heat transfer characteristics as cast-iron stoves of the same thickness, and they can withstand high firebox temperatures equally well without cracking. Some steel stoves come with replaceable steel or firebrick liners to help prevent burnout.

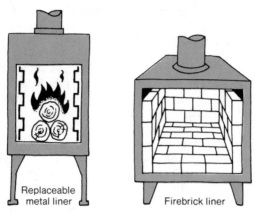

Replaceable metal liner

Firebrick liner

Firebrick and steel liners *are used to extend the useful life of a stove.*

Disadvantages. Warping can be a problem, especially with the lighter gauge stoves. Overfiring a steel stove may cause it to warp. A slight warp probably won't affect the performance of a steel stove, but it will affect the appearance. More serious warping may cause the doors to fit improperly or break welds, causing the stove to lose its airtightness. Some steel stoves have cylindrical or oval designs to help keep this warping to a minimum.

What to look for. As with cast-iron stoves, check steel stoves for airtightness. Make sure doors fit properly, no parts are missing, and everything works. Check the welds to make sure they are uniform and continuous; poor welds are pitted or uneven.

Ease of operation

When you're shopping for a stove, such conveniences as ash pans, insulated door handles, and large loading doors may seem relatively unimportant factors in making your selection. However, if you operate your stove on a regular basis, you will learn to appreciate the importance of these "little" conveniences.

Loading wood

Stoves with large fireboxes naturally accept larger chunks of wood, provided the pieces fit through the loading door. A large firebox and a large loading door mean less work chopping and splitting wood. Even in small stoves, the size of the loading door should be in proportion to the firebox size.

Location of loading doors. The loading door on a stove is located on either the front or the top of the stove. Many of the "top loaders" have a tendency to puff smoke into the room when the door or lid is opened. The same thing may happen with front loaders if the loading door is too large for the firebox size. On front-loading stoves, make sure the door is at a convenient height. If the door on the stove is too low, you'll have to stoop to load the wood unless you place the stove on a raised hearth.

When smoke gets in your eyes: *it may be a problem with some top-loading stoves.*

Basketball player's nightmare: *small stoves with low doors should be placed on raised hearth.*

Door handles. The door handle on a stove should be easy to operate. When checking stoves, open and shut each door a few times; you should not have to force a door shut in order to make it seal tight. Also, the door handle should be insulated or located where it will not overheat. Some door handles get too hot to touch after the stove has been operating a few hours; if so, you may have to keep a heavy glove handy to open the door. If your stove dealer knows his product, he'll be able to tell you how hot the handle gets. The same holds true with damper controls, though air inlet controls tend not to get as hot as door handles because cool air is passing over them on its way into the firebox.

Ash removal

Removing the ashes from a stove can be a messy job, so ask your dealer how often this chore must be done. If you can, choose a stove with a large ash holding capacity. Inspect the stove to see how easy it will be to remove the ashes. The stove should have a large ash lip to keep ashes from falling on the hearth. Some stoves come equipped with removable ash pans, making ash removal neater and easier. If your stove doesn't have this convenience you'll need a scuttle and shovel, along with a broom, to clean up the mess (see "Stove accessories," page 30).

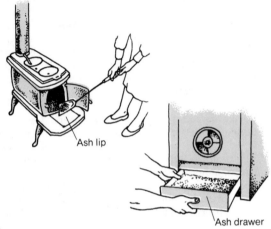

Ash lip

Ash drawer

Ash removal aids *include large ash lip (left) to keep ashes off hearth, ash removal pan (right)*

Other conveniences & features

Some stoves have features that are not necessarily related to their ease of operation but, nonetheless, add much to the pleasure of having a wood stove.

Glass doors and windows. Part of the romance of fireplaces and Franklin stoves is being able to gaze into the flames, so a number of stoves have glass doors or windows of various sizes that at least give you a peek at the fire inside. The glass in these stoves should be tempered and the panes should fit loosely to allow for expansion; otherwise they'll crack. But if the panes do have a loose fit, some of the stove's air-tightness may be sacrificed. And remember that the glass must be cleaned frequently to remove soot and creosote deposits. Nevertheless, the feeling of warmth you get from seeing the fire may well be worth it to you.

Cooking on the stove

Just about every stove has at least enough room on top for a tea kettle; but some of the stoves used primarily for heating have larger cooking surfaces than others. Those that accommodate several pots and pans will allow you to prepare simple meals in the event of an emergency. Cookstoves (see drawing, page 4), though used primarily for cooking, make good radiant heaters, and contribute a surprising amount of heat to the house. Kitchen ranges, on the other hand, are usually insulated to retain oven heat and restrict surface heat to the cooking area; but they will contribute some heat to the room they're in. See page 84 for a discussion of kitchen ranges.

Box stoves and box-type stove designs usually offer the largest cooking surfaces. If you plan to do any cooking on your stove, it should have at least one pot hole with a removable lid, and a separate handle for removing the lid when you want to cook directly over the fire.

Pothole lid *on box stove is removed for cooking directly over the fire.*

Paints & finishes

Black is the traditional color for stoves because it was considered the best color for radiating heat and the easiest color to maintain. For years and years, cast-iron stoves were treated with a solution of stove black or stove polish which had to be applied annually to maintain the stove's appearance. Today, however, most cast-iron and steel stoves are painted with a flat, black, high-temperature enamel finish, though some of the cast-iron ones may still require the annual "stove blackings."

There are a few stoves available in a limited range of colors, usually in baked enamel finishes. Kitchen ranges and modern circulating heaters may have either baked enamel or porcelain enamel finishes.

For touch-ups, you can buy stove polish and spray cans of high-temperature enamel in most hardware stores or from your stove dealer.

Stove accessories

No wood stove is complete without its accessories. Those shown here are but a few of the many available, and they range from simple firetending tools to complicated heat exchangers. One or more may be perfect for your stove.

Firetending tools. A basic set of firetending tools is a useful accessory to any wood stove. You probably won't need your tongs and poker as much as you would with a fireplace, since wood stove fires require little tending, but the shovel will be useful to remove ashes. Be sure you have a shovel that fits the door to your stove. If you have a box stove, you might also find an ash hoe useful for raking coals to the front of the stove for the morning's fire.

Ash removal aids. No one likes to carry out ashes, but it has to be done periodically, even with very efficient stoves. Several manufacturers make trays and boxes designed to aid in ash removal. Or perhaps that decorative coal scuttle you've had for years can be pressed into service.

Log carriers and woodboxes. Simple metal or canvas log carriers are a great help when it's time to haul in the next load of wood. They not only allow you to carry more, they make the job neater and they also look good on the hearth once the wood is inside. Boxes, barrels, baskets, coal scuttles and the like—all make attractive and practical additions to your stove installation.

Stove polish and paint. Unless your stove has a porcelain enamel surface, you will occasionally need to renew the finish. Heat and moisture tend to discolor matte-finish stoves, but a little polish or paint will make them look like new. Polish comes in tubes or bottles and is applied with a rag. High-temperature paints come in a range of colors, usually in aerosol cans. You may need to remove your stove before you do touch-up spraying, or at least mask the hearth in order to protect it from the overspray.

Add-on ovens and shelves. If you want to use your stove for baking and warming food, you might consider adding an oven or shelf. A stove or freestanding fireplace with a high flue temperature will profit from the addition of a flue oven designed to replace one of the sections of the flue pipe. If you have a more efficient stove, with a lower flue temperature, you should probably use a stove-top oven to avoid overcooling the flue.

All ovens and warming shelves add useful radiant surface area to your stove, increasing its heating capacity. For more information, see "Cooking with your wood stove," page 92.

Heat exchangers. These are designed to boost the heating capacity of your stove and flue by increasing their radiant surface area, increasing the amount of air moving over the hot surfaces, or both. But although heat exchangers may benefit many stoves and freestanding fireplaces, they are not for everybody. See "Heat-recovery devices," page 21, for more information.

Water coils and jackets. These add-ons have been on the wood-heat scene for years; they can make your wood stove more convenient and useful. Available in a wide range of designs, and often custom-built, they require the aid of a competent installer if safety is to be assured.

With these devices, many wood stoves are capable of supplying all of a family's hot water needs, and the hot water can also be used to heat rooms other than the one in which the stove is installed. See "Heat-recovery devices," page 21, and "Hot water systems," page 91, for more information.

Smoke detectors and fire extinguishers. You may not normally view these as stove accessories, but every wood stove owner should give them serious thought. The Uniform Building Code now requires smoke detectors in new construction, and their use is especially important if you are heating with wood. A good smoke detector and fire extinguisher are certainly worth their cost in peace of mind—and they are indispensable should an emergency arise.

Stove accessories are an integral part of the setting for your wood stove. You can combine their utilitarian and decorative functions in a way that is uniquely your own.

Firetending tools

Wood storage items

Stoneware crock

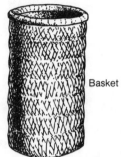

Basket

Metal log carrier

Canvas log carrier

Ash removal aids

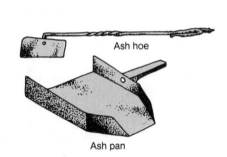

Coal scuttle

Ash hoe

Ash pan

Heat recovery devices

Chimney fins

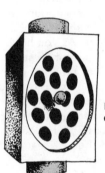

Heat exchanger

Flue pipe add-ons

Flue oven

Warming shelf

Old-time ceiling fan

Wood Stoves in Color

Wood stoves represent more than a charming touch of nostalgia—they are an old idea capable of meeting today's urgent need for alternative energy sources in home heating. Today, as they did more than a century ago, wood stoves are warming homes, cooking meals, and contributing to a self-sufficient life style. One or more stoves can supplement a conventional heating system or can be the primary source of heat in the house.

If you're thinking of a wood stove, begin your shopping here. As you browse through the next 31 pages, you may be pleasantly surprised at the variety of stoves available; they range from antiques and their reproductions to unique stoves of modern design. This color gallery features stoves of many shapes, sizes, and colors. In each instance, the stove has been pleasingly integrated with the decor of the home. You'll find installations for every room of the house, ideas to consider for adapting to your own situation.

Freestanding enameled stove pro
plenty of warmth for the lofty,
spaces of this kitchen/dining/li
area. Lacking interior walls, the r
is ideally suited for radiant v
heat, and the stove add
attractive focal p
Design: Edward K

Which Stove for You?

Discover a variety of styles

Wood stoves are bewildering in their variety. From the basic Franklin stove (which is really somewhere between a stove and a fireplace) to baffled airtight designs, the market offers something for every taste—and budget. Your stove can be a purely functional unit or can double as a decorative focal point of a room; you can cook on it, heat water with it, or simply enjoy its warmth. Although these photos show only some of the many types available, they will give you an introduction to today's world of wood heating.

△
Small in stature, this cast-iron box stove is ideally suited for a corner installation. Though with its simple slide drafts it isn't airtight, the box stove is a thrifty choice.

△
A tradition for generations, the Franklin fireplace has warmed America's homes and hearts for more than 150 years.

Circular sliding doors on this modern Scandinavian stove ▷ offer airtight burning when closed. When open, the stove accommodates a screen for safe burning while you enjoy the fire. Design: Larry Olson

△
Welded, steel-plate construction of this simple airtight stove makes installing coils for water heating an easy job. Heated water is piped to holding tank located in the attic.

△
Scandinavian arch tops this stove's firebox. The surface area added by this arch boosts heat output considerably.

△
Small fingers won't be burned by this steel-jacketed circulating stove. Air travels between the firebox and the jacket and rises as it is heated, creating convection currents.

Compact kitchen range has ▷ been in production since the turn of the century. In addition to standard oven and cookplates, it features warming oven and tank for heating and storing water.

△
Classic Franklin, an old standby, has endured the passage of time. Though not air tight, the Franklin burns as a heater with its doors closed or, with doors open, as a fireplace.

These stoves let you view the fire

If you enjoy the charm of watching an open fire, yet are interested in real heating efficiency, you might want to consider a stove with front doors that can be left open during use, or one with a glass front. Either type allows you to have your cake and heat it too. Of course, when stove doors are left open, heating efficiency is sacrificed. Though glass-fronted units allow a continual view of the fire without heat loss, glass cleaning will become one of your firetending chores.

△
Heat output belies its size. This small Scandinavian stove's doors open—or even come off—for enjoying the fire, but with doors closed, it generates a surprising quantity of heat.

An air-tight stove in disguise, this adaptation of the Franklin design features fireview doors that allow airtight operation when closed, thermostatic draft controls, and baffles for circulating convection currents around its surface.
▽

Space-age octagonal fireplace/stove combination ▷ circulates heat with a built-in fan and draws outside combustion air through a special duct. Because it has a "zero clearance" rating, you can put it next to combustible surfaces. In addition, it is approved for installation in mobile homes.

△

Handsome arc of this stove complements practically any interior with its simplicity of form. Removable glass door, hinged at the bottom, lets you enjoy the fire while keeping precious heat from escaping up the flue. Architect: Jerry Tierney.

◁ **Flip-up glass door** fronts this straightforward stove and makes fire tending easy. To protect the glass from heat shock when fire is first lit, a metal shield swings in front of it. The switch in front controls a blower that circulates heat away from stove. Design: Mike Booth.

△
Victorian embossed cast-iron box stove has warmed three generations of its owner's family. Small enough to transport easily from one location to another, it now resides aboard a converted Navy launch.

Antiques: real and reproduced

Wood stoves have come a very long way since Grandma and Grandpa used them for cooking and heating. However, the best designs of yesteryear have survived the passage of time, and many reproductions are available.

Here are a few of yesterday's stoves that are solving some of today's energy problems. Some are antiques; one is a replica. As you can see, most are as decorative as they are hard-working.

Vintage 1887, this ornate, side-loading parlor stove provides the ▷ perch for a 300-year-old Japanese incense-burning crow. Six-inch-thick concrete and exposed aggregate hearth mediates the transition between the old stove and the room's contemporary decor.

◁ **Lovingly restored** and replated parlor stove commands attention as the central focus in this living room. Both room and hearth were designed with the stove in mind. High ceiling allows ample space for the stove's 6-foot stature.

◁ **Since 1910,** a wood stove has warmed this houseboat and charmed its residents and guests. This antique stove's simple hearth of handmade stoneware tiles adds color and character to its setting.

△
A proud imposter, this "antique" wood stove is actually a reproduction. For its hearth, the stove uses the house's tile floor. To take advantage of its full heating capacity, it stands in an open area just off the entry and living room.

△
Antique lines of this restored parlor stove contrast effectively with the contemporary feel of this bedroom. Stove furnishes cozy heat for bedroom and accompanying bath.

...Antiques

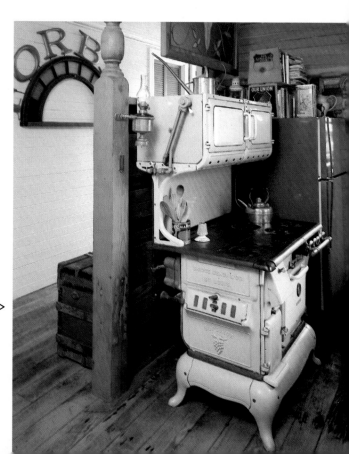

Hardworking antique range cooks all of the meals in this ▷ houseboat's kitchen and helps purge the morning chill. Typical of stoves made between 1910 and 1925, it is fueled partly by gas and partly by wood.

△
Timeworn but operable, this venerable box stove warms the breakfast
room in a hurry on cool mornings. Rather than build a separate hearth,
the owners took advantage of the tile floor for its base.

◁ **As though from Captain Nemo's
depths,** this ornate stove bridges
the gap between fantasy and
functionalism. Found in an old attic,
it is an antiquer's dream come true.
The extensive view of the fire that it
offers is unusual and quite distinctive.

△
Glass all around turns this freestanding fireplace into a relatively efficient heater. The large hood and flue contribute significantly to its radiant heat output. Draft between glass panes swirls fire and helps keep glass clean. Stones in hearth were reclaimed from owner's property.

Freestanding fireplaces

For roasting marshmallows or romancing by the fire, freestanding fireplaces outshine most of their more efficient cousins, the wood stoves. With freestanding fireplaces you can see and enjoy the fire—something you cannot do with many wood stoves.

These fireplaces are available in just about every color and finish under the sun, offering tremendous decorative variety. As with an open masonry fireplace, though, you'll burn more wood than with a stove (see page 11).

◁ **Diminutive size** makes this freestanding fireplace ideal for heating a single room. Note that to avoid penetrating the valance above, the flue pipe vents out through the wall. The handsome hearth is of ceramic tile. Architect: Leonard E. Lincoln.

△ Heat is stored in the cast-concrete inner lining of this handsome freestanding fireplace. Finishes available include several porcelain enamel colors and—for high budgets—polished metals such as chrome.

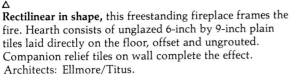

△
Rectilinear in shape, this freestanding fireplace frames the fire. Hearth consists of unglazed 6-inch by 9-inch plain tiles laid directly on the floor, offset and ungrouted. Companion relief tiles on wall complete the effect. Architects: Ellmore/Titus.

Basic conical fireplace has become a modern classic. ▷ Having given rise to most of the other fireplaces pictured here, this one still finds a place in many homes. Flexible in installation and relatively inexpensive, this freestanding fireplace—like most—is considerably more heat-efficient than a standard masonry fireplace.

43

Designs for Wood Heat

Homes planned around the stove

If you are planning a new home and considering heating it with a wood stove, keep a few points in mind while developing your plans. Place the stove in a central location, allowing for a flue and any venting or ducting equipment; plan for open spaces between levels and for a minimum of walls. The key is to allow the heat an unobstructed path to all of your home's spaces (see page 16).

Passive systems, shown on this page, let heated air rise from the stove and flow freely through the house (the stove must be placed on a lower level). Active systems (on the facing page) usually employ fans and ductwork to circulate heat throughout the house.

△

High lofts, interior chimney, and double glazing provide for efficient circulation and retention of heat from both sun and large wood stove. Heat-exchanger arch built into stove has doors enclosing an oven, allowing the stove to do double duty. Architects: Davies Bibbins Menders.

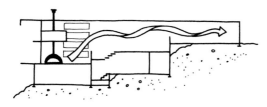

Stove's heat travels from lower-level living room to upper-level bedroom in this solar house with wood heat back-up. Smart contemporary stove and long east wall with large windows combine for quick heating in the morning; tile stores warmth from both sun and stove during the day. Architects: Ellmore/Titus.
▽

◁ **Geodesic dome house** is well-adapted for heating with this powerful stove/fireplace combination. Heat moves upward through two lofts, collects, and is ducted down to rear bedrooms on the main floor and first loft. Tile backing for the stove was a challenge for the tile setter, but his efforts paid off with a design that complements both the lines of the stove and the structure of the house. Design: Scott Salsbury.

◁ **Heat climbs the stairs** and is ducted to other rooms in this wood-heated home. A fan in floor vent on upper landing returns cool air to the stove for reheating. The used-brick hearth retains heat in its mass, provides a place for storing firewood to right of stove. Design: Jackson and Kimberly Jane Davis, Mike Booth.

Open trusses are both dramatic and ▷ functional in this house heated entirely by the stove seen here. The high-ceilinged space forms a natural "lake" of warm air; a powered ducting system taps this supply and forces heat to the basement and bedrooms. Freestanding brick wall dividing the living space is warmed by the stove, then radiates its stored heat to the dining room and kitchen beyond. Design: Paul Korhummel.

Remodeling with a stove in mind

Installing a hearth or putting in a flue is usually a much more manageable job if you're remodeling. Of course, this depends upon the extent of your work, but if walls and ceilings are open and your house is torn up anyway, the time is right for adding a wood stove. If you work out a good remodeling plan, you can provide for spaces that are easy to heat, and you can allow for such features as convenient wood storage or heat circulating systems.

△

Stove in alcove is the primary heater for this remodeled bungalow; gas-wood range adds supplemental heat, as well as doing the cooking. Alcove guides heated air to pair of registers above stove (left). Upper register allows air to convect to children's bedrooms in attic; lower register opens to duct system powered by blower in closet behind alcove. Ducts continue under floor to main living and working spaces (see plan, below). House has solar back-up system designed to keep the chill off when the stove isn't operating. Design: Frank Verprauskus, Dean Metcalf.

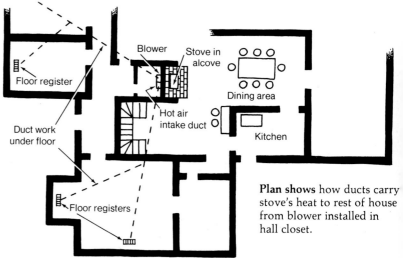

Plan shows how ducts carry stove's heat to rest of house from blower installed in hall closet.

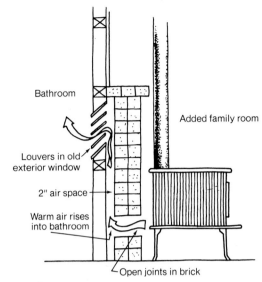

Family room and bath are heated by small box stove in custom-designed brick alcove with built-in convection system (see plan, right). Detachable screen locks firmly in place in front of the stove, protecting children from the stove's hot surfaces (see inset), yet still allows clearance for stoking. Design: Steve Bowers, Bob Burnside.

Bathroom

Added family room

Louvers in old exterior window

2" air space

Warm air rises into bathroom

Open joints in brick

△

Two-inch air space behind brick hearth allows air to rise through louvered opening (it once was an exterior window) into bathroom.

Historic structure, originally built in the early 1700s, has ▷ been by turns a fish house, a squash warehouse, and a theater that Eugene O'Neill once used. Now it's a home. The present owner erected a large hearth for fireplace and stove and built lofts above it. Brick chimney surrounds the stove's metal flue, funneling heat into the open spaces above. Design: Lawrence E. Murphy.

△
Energy-efficient add-on garden room is solar heated; a wood stove supplements the sun's heat. Porcelainized cast-iron stove echoes the traditional design of European tile stoves. The room's hexagonal floor tiles continue under the stove, becoming the hearth. Architects: Johnson Olney Associates.

An easy way to heat an add-on

Wood stoves are often an economical answer to heating add-on rooms. Because they offer localized heat remote from the house's primary heating system, you have maximum control of heat in the addition, independent of the main house. Unlike forced-air furnaces, which are usually awkward to extend, wood stoves can be installed relatively simply in most additions. And unlike electric heaters, which are quite expensive to use, wood stoves offer economical heat.

Family room add-on is heated by small Scandinavian ▷ airtight, baffled box stove. Extremely efficient for its size, this stove handles the job easily. Tile-faced wall protection is vented on sides and top to allow air circulation.

He's cozy while he reads by this small, powerful ▷
stove in a solarium built between house and
garage. The steel shroud over cast-iron firebox
protects against burns. This stove is available in
many decorator colors.

◁ **Freestanding fireplace** sufficiently heats small room
added between garage and house. Ceramic tile floor
extends under fireplace to provide a hearth. Shields
on fireplace guide convection currents; they are
available in many contrasting colors.

Successful Installations

All through the house

Imagine drifting off to sleep to the sound of a crackling fire, or picture bathing by the warmth of a woodburning stove. No matter where you put one, a woodburning stove creates relaxing moods. Here are a few examples of stoves in out-of-the-mainstream locations.

△

Bathside antique stove, sitting directly on tile floor, warms bathers, dries towels, makes bathing all the more pleasurable space saver, this stove is ideal for small rooms.

Modern counterpart of the French stove at right is the functional and elegant one below. Placed in a dining room that was added long ago, but never adequately heated, this stove's flue plugs into the back of an existing fireplace. Design: Steve Berman.

▽

◁ **Built into a bedroom fireplace,** this stove has doors that allow viewing the fire while reading in bed. It heats both the bedroom and an adjoining bath.

△
Small combination fireplace/stove is centrally located in a lofty second-story bedroom. A fan-powered duct on the wall above it (not shown) carries warm air to the first-floor rooms.

...try to teen's bedroom ▷ ...oubles as a hearth for ...l stove. Muddy tracks and dirt clean easily ...from tile; wet clothes, hung by stove, dry quickly. Traditional Scandinavian arch ...eatly increases stove's ...at output. Architects: Ellmore/Titus.

Heating attics and basements

Attics and basements receive more than their share of remodeling when the crunch for space hits. Yet because they are like add-ons, they are often cut off from a house's primary heating system. For this reason, they are likely candidates for wood stoves.

Remember that flues must extend above the roof line, as required by code. In an attic, this is usually no problem; but in the basement of a three-story house—unless the stove can be connected to an existing unused flue—it may be nearly impossible. In such a case, seek professional advice.

Lavishly remodeled attic studio displays an elegant, ▷ enameled Scandinavian arch stove that stands on a custom-made oval, marble hearth. Flue is standard insulated pipe wrapped in a copper sheath. Design: Creative Spaces.

Attic sitting room is amply heated by ▷ Danish steel stove with sliding door that permits use as either a fireplace or semiairtight stove. Hearth of ½-inch-thick steel sits flush with flooring, on top of insulating material, and continues up the wall and across the ceiling. The steel backing, set out by noncombustible spacers, is bolted through wallboard to studs. The steel is painted with stove black. Architects: Davies Bibbins Menders.

Remodeled basement is amply heated by this fireview stove. Flue penetrates wall. With its cathedral-style doors open, the stove serves as a fireplace; with doors closed, the stove becomes an efficient heater.
Architects: Unihab Inc.

◁ **Compact basement dining/study area** is heated by a space-saving enameled iron stove. Some of this stove's heat rises upstairs to the remainder of the apartment. Architects: Davies Bibbins.

Wood stoves in kitchens

If the kitchen is the heart of a house, the stove is what keeps it ticking. Here we show a variety of kitchens equipped with wood stoves. Some are used for cooking, some are not.

Incidentally, wood range owners say that because their ovens are unvented, baked food loses none of its flavor and aroma. Conventional ranges, they say, can't compare.

One thing to keep in mind regarding wood cook stoves: unless a stove is insulated, it will take only one hot summer day to teach you what slaving over a hot stove is all about.

Heating kitchen and eating area, firebrick-lined ▷ French upright stove does double duty as a space heater and a stove that's used for back-up cooking and keeping dishes warm. Decorative tile hearth with contrasting border complements the stove. Architect: Thomas Amsler.

Original to this kitchen, wood range dates back ▷ over a century. Though it is now supplemented by a modern range, stoves like this one once were the sole means of cooking.

This wood-burning range turns out many of the family's meals, especially breakfasts. Supplementing the modern cooking facilities in the kitchen on the other side of the wall, this antique stove stands in a solar-heated eating area, giving the house an extra heating boost.
Architects: Ellmore/Titus.

Utilitarian kitchen exploits this cast-iron modern American airtight stove. The stove does double duty, contributing both heat and back-up cooking. The exaggerated bas reliefs on its sides substantially increase its surface area, awarding a heating bonus. Inside the stove, reversible liners change firebox size—you use one size for heavy-duty winter burning, the other for small spring and fall fires.

Wood heat to work by

Workshops, studios, and other detached work spaces usually come out on the short end of the priorities when heat gets doled out in a house. Since these spaces are located away from the main living quarters, extending an existing heating system is often an expensive proposition.

Wood heat can be a solution. Wood stoves are cozy to work by, enable you to keep a hot cup of coffee nearby, and lend a special air to the creative atmosphere.

△
Centrally located small box stove heats artist's studio and adjacent sitting area. Simple long flue pipe adds significantly to the radiant surface area , increasing the amount of heat transmitted to the room.

△
Small office is heated by antique pot-belly stove. A classic, this type once heated railway stations. The stove's hearth is of quarry tile.

△
Tapestry studio is part of a converted parking garage. The building's concrete structure made conventional heating nearly impossible. A wood stove was installed relatively easily, especially because the concrete floor didn't require a separate hearth. The stove heats the large space quite well and adds to the charm of the decor.

△
In a potter's studio, this wood stove's continuous heat output keeps him warm and dries his pots while he works. With the ash hoe in the foreground, he rakes coals forward in the morning for easy lighting of the fire.

When space is in short supply

A stove on a large hearth can be the dominant focal point in a room, but this may not be for you. Sometimes there is a need for subtlety, or at least compactness, in a stove installation.

On these pages we feature stoves tucked away in corners on small hearths that do not dominate the room. These installations de-emphasize the stove while saving space in the room. One of these installations even has a demountable hearth—both stove and hearth are removed during the warm months.

△

Out of the mainstream, glass-fronted stove maintains a low profile in this family room. Raised hearth permits easy loading through side door and puts the fire in better view.

△

Heating a small study and adjacent bedroom, combination air-tight stove/fireplace requires minimum space because it is compact and mostly vertical in dimension. Floor-to-ceiling tile provides a useful thermal mass, storing heat for gradual release. Architect: John Cole.

◁ **This stove takes a summer vacation.** When the warm summer months hit, the owners move the stove out of their small-space living room. Lightweight and compact, the stove is easily moved. The hearth, consisting of tile laid on removable panels, detaches from the wall, lifts from the floor, and stores flat.

In a mobile home, this plate-steel stove satisfies strict federal safety requirements. It draws outdoor combustion air through its pedestal base and is approved for minimum clearance to combustible surfaces. Hearth is easily installed one-piece synthetic material.
▽

△
Diminutive box stove, well adapted to small-space situations, sits in a corner of this breakfast room. For minimum clearance between stove and walls, a ventilation space separates brick from fire-rated wallboard. Design: Warren A. Burtis.

△
Large fireplace such as this one can house an entire wood stove. Damper assembly was removed and replaced by a steel plate through which the flue pipe was run.

Converting the fireplace

Do you have a heat-wasting, wood-wasting fireplace that you would like to reform? Consider converting it to receive a wood stove. By taking advantage of the existing flue and hearth, you could cut the cost of a wood stove installation by more than half, yet keep a fireplace facade that may be too good to give up. Some stoves fit right into the fireplace's opening (see page 10), others sit partially in and partially out (for more heat radiation), and many can sit on the hearth or a hearth extension. For more about fireplace conversions, see page 76.

Elegant fireplace facade was saved, despite the fact that the fireplace ▷ was an energy waster, by placing a wood stove on a hearth extension in front of it. Heat is deflected away from the woodwork by an angled metal plate inside the fireplace opening.

◁ **Stove sits sideways** on this hearth, eliminating the need for a hearth extension and saving space. This stove's sculptured side harmoniously echoes the tile's forest motif.

Large, drafty room, previously unused because fireplace stole its heat, is now warmed by a stove that sits in the fireplace opening. When stove doors are open, guests enjoy the flickering flames.
▽

Completely rebuilt to receive a stove, this fireplace was reconstructed from its original brick. The brick retains the heat from the stove, radiating it back into the room. Stove's doors open to reveal the fire.
Design: Hubert A. Kay.
▽

Hearths: For a custom touch

Every wood stove needs a hearth of one kind or another. The hearth gives a stove its support and protects the area around the stove from fire. Hearths can be designed to retain a stove's heat for later release, to redirect radiant heat from the stove, or to do something as simple as store wood.

The design of the hearth, in both material and form, gives you a chance to put your artistry and imagination to work. The sampling on these pages offers some ideas for creating effective and decorative hearths. Of course, you can draw ideas for hearths from nearly all of the photos in this book.

◁ **Reflective copper backing** bounces heat from this stove back into the room. Flat 1-foot by 6-foot copper sheets were crimped with ½-inch-high standing seams on 5-inch centers in a metal shop. Behind the copper is an insulating backing, then air space, then the wallboard. Because the hearth is raised, its massiveness is minimized. Architect: K. Peter Braun.

△
Decorative handmade designer tile adorns this wall. The stove has a shield along its back, permitting closer clearance to the wall. Flue exits directly behind the stove, straight out the wall and up the house's exterior. This side-loading stove has thermostatically controlled draft inlets.

△
In this passive solar home, the Mexican floor tile is the hearth for retaining the heat from both sun and stove. Used brick wall divides the kitchen from the main living area, radiates heat. Loft area above is also heated by the stove.

rving brick wall makes the stove a focal point in this solar
ne's living room, and directs its radiant heat to the living
ce. Storage cabinets flank the hearth on both sides. This and
e other wood stove provide all of the back-up for the solar
ting. Architects: G. Cichanski & Associates.

△

Freestanding brick wall radiates stove's heat from both sides,
defines stairway, and acts as a room divider. From this location,
heat flows easily into the primary living areas. Heat pump
circulates heat throughout remainder of house.
Design: Bruce Fix.

△
Pair of arches frames both the stove and stored wood.
This stove is located in the home's basement—heat flows
up through a vent directly above the stove to the rest of
the house. Custom-made black iron flue angles from
stove to the main flue. Design: Kristine King.

Raised adobe hearth stores a week's worth of wood below, ▷
makes stove easier to load and cook on. Material on wall
behind the stove is insulating board, spaced 1 inch away
from the wallboard and painted white.
Design: Betsy Wilson and Ev Banfield.

HEARTHS **63**

Living
with
Your Stove

○ INSTALLING YOUR STOVE

○ USING YOUR STOVE

○ A WOODCHOPPER'S GUIDE

uying your stove is just the first step in your venture into the world of wood heat. Next come the challenges of designing an attractive installation for your new stove, learning to fire and maintain the stove properly, and to select, season, and store your wood supply.

This section takes up these questions and more. You'll learn how to design a safe, legal stove installation—or where to go for professional assistance should you decide not to tackle the job yourself. You'll find out about chimneys: their design, building, renovation, and maintenance. There's advice on fire building that instructs you on how to fire your stove and control its heat output. And finally, the "Woodchopper's Guide" offers information on selecting, cutting, seasoning, and storing wood.

The following pages get down to the real business of heating with wood, the day-to-day ins and outs of life with a wood stove.

Installing Your Stove

Stove, hearth and chimney constitute the triad of stove installation—the latter two comprise the bulk of work involved. You have the option of tackling one or all three of these phases: installing the chimney, building the hearth, or simply placing the stove on a professionally built hearth and connecting it to the chimney. The following pages serve as a practical guide for planning and executing each phase of installation.

Planning the installation

Once you've bought your stove and chosen its location in the house, you can plan your hearth and chimney installation. You can choose from a variety of hearth styles and masonry materials—you might find something in the color section of this book that suits your taste and be able to adapt it to your situation. Stove dealers, installers, and masons can suggest a layout or help you if you want to design your own hearth.

The type of chimney you install and the required materials will depend on your house design and the location of your stove in the house.

Who installs it?

Safe installation of a stove's hearth and chimney can be tricky and often is best left to a professional. A reputable stove installer will be familiar with local building codes and safe installation practices, and you can depend on him to secure necessary permits, estimate materials, and help you plan a safe, efficient installation.

If, however, you feel competent enough to do the installation yourself and wish to tackle the job, first read the remainder of this chapter so you're fully aware of what's involved before you make your decision. Pay special attention to the sections on stove and flue pipe clearances, recommended hearth and chimney materials, and building permits. If you do run into any problems installing the stove or chimney or have questions regarding the safety of your installation, don't hesitate to seek professional help.

Working with an installer. A reputable stove dealer will either have his own installation crew or be able to recommend a reliable installer or general contractor to do the job. Many brick and stone masons are experienced in hearth installation and will be able to offer custom hearth designs in various masonry materials or build a hearth to your specifications.

Before contracting a job with an installer, make sure he carries liability insurance on his work. If you should have a fire and it can be traced directly to a faulty installation, the installer's insurance company will cover resulting damages.

Many installers will guarantee their work against defects in workmanship (usually for a period of 6 months to a year after installation). Under the guarantee, the installer is responsible for repairing the chimney should it leak or fall apart. Ask the installer exactly what the guarantee covers. The installer can seldom guarantee that the chimney will draw properly because it's often difficult to determine the effect of geographical location and local weather conditions on chimney draft. An experienced installer, though, should be familiar with these conditions and take them into account when he installs the chimney. If the chimney doesn't draw properly once it's installed, it may require an additional length of pipe on the top or a special chimney cap (see "Chimney installation," page 71).

Getting bids. Unless purchase price of your stove includes installation, you should attempt to get several bids on the installation work. If you're using a mason who does custom hearth work, you'll probably be getting separate bids on hearth and chimney installations. When you get a bid, find out what work and materials are included. A reputable installer will give you a bid in writing and list all materials, their prices, and a price for services performed. Because prices on materials and labor are continually rising, it's a good idea to find out when the bid expires and get the expiration date in writing. For instance, one installer may give you a bid that is good for 30 days from date of issue, allowing you that amount of time to get competitive bids before his prices are subject to change. Some installers will work on a per-hour basis, charging you for the amount of time it takes to do the installation. If you go this route, you will probably have to obtain the building permit and provide the necessary materials. Unless the installer is insured or bonded (financially capable of accepting liability for his work), you will be held legally responsible for the safety of the installation.

Contracts. The agreement you make with an installer should be spelled out in a final written contract. The contract should include a complete list of materials and services, a completion date, guarantees on work and follow-up services, and a payment schedule. A good contract protects both you and the installer should either of you fail to meet its specified terms.

Installing it yourself. If you plan to do your own installation, the first task is to develop a detailed set of plans to go with your application for a building permit. Your plans should include the exact location of stove and chimney, hearth details, and a list of all hearth and chimney materials used in the installation. After you've presented your plans to the local building department and obtained a permit, work can begin. For most amateur builders, the easiest sequence is to build the hearth first and then install the chimney. This minimizes the amount of time you have a hole open to the weather.

Safety is the watchword in wood stove installation! Many destructive house fires are caused by improper installation or a faulty chimney. Make sure you are thoroughly familiar with recommended clearances and proper installation materials and procedures before you start.

Determining stove placement

Once you've chosen a location for your stove, you must determine the stove's exact position within that location. When placing the stove, you'll have to take into consideration the required clearances for stove and stovepipe from combustible surfaces, and the best location for the chimney outlet in the room.

Keep in mind that the chimney and chimney connection should be as vertical as possible, minimizing horizontal runs, bends, or offsets that restrict draft. The chimney connection includes all components used inside the room with the stove to connect the stove to the chimney. The chimney itself includes all pipe, masonry, and components used outside the stove room to vent the smoke outdoors. If you're venting the stove into an existing fireplace or unused chimney, the placement of the stove will be restricted by the location of the chimney or fireplace opening.

If you're installing a new chimney, first decide where the chimney will run (see page 69); then locate the chimney opening in the wall or ceiling as close as possible to the intended stove position. For information on possible chimney locations, see "Chimney installation" on page 71.

It should be mentioned at this point that a stove should never be placed in a closet, alcove, or other enclosed area. Even with the prescribed safe clearances, a stove in one of these areas not only radiates less heat into the room but is also a potential fire hazard. One exception might be a stove that is provided with an adequate fan or duct system that efficiently transfers accumulated heat to other parts of the house. An example of this type of installation appears on page 46 in the color section. If you're interested in such an installation, consult your local building department to see if it meets code requirements in your area.

Stove and stovepipe clearances

One of the prime requirements for a safe stove installation is that you place the stove and stovepipe a safe distance from all combustible materials (furniture, wood storage, etc.) and surfaces (floors, walls, ceilings, cabinets, etc.). In addition, you must provide adequate floor protection around the stove in the event that glowing embers or other burning material fall from the stove.

The National Fire Protection Association (NFPA) recommends differing minimum safe clearances and installation standards for both radiant and circulating wood stoves and heaters. Radiant stoves have single wall fireboxes and heat primarily by radiation. Circulating stoves and heaters circulate air through an outer jacket around the firebox and their resultant cooler surface allows them to be placed closer to combustible surfaces. See page 11 for a discussion of the two types. These NFPA standards have been adopted by most building departments across the country and the stove industry as a whole. These clearances should be followed unless the stove manufacturer's instructions specify otherwise.

Some radiant stoves come equipped with heat shields or are designed so they may be placed closer to combustibles than the minimum required distance for radiant heaters. Other stoves may require clearances that exceed NFPA recommendations. The manufacturers of these stoves usually include recommended minimum safe distances in the installation instructions. For all other radiant stoves, refer to the drawing below for required stove and stovepipe clearances. Radiant stoves should have a minimum of 36 inches clearance from combustible walls, ceilings, and all combustible materials.

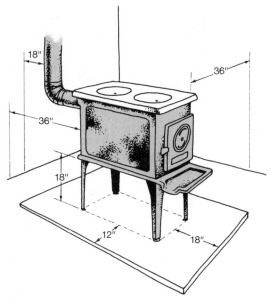

Use these clearances *for radiant stoves without listed clearance requirements; first check local codes.*

Clearance from the bottom of the stove need only be 18 inches; however, all combustible floors must be covered with a noncombustible hearth material as shown in the drawing above. Noncombustible materials include brick, tile, other types of masonry, noncombustible simulated masonry, metal, and stoveboard. Floor protection must be continuous—bricks or stone must be mortared, tile must be grouted, and so on. The floor hearth must extend 18 inches beyond the loading door side of the stove (usually the front) and 12 inches beyond the other two sides and back. The clearance from the bottom of the stove body to the floor can be reduced if an approved insulating stoveboard or hearth material is used.

The chart on the facing page gives the minimum NFPA-recommended clearances for radiant stoves, along with those for wood-burning kitchen ranges, circulating stoves, and chimney connector pipe. The figures are recommended only for stoves unaccompanied by manufacturer's recommended clearances. Make sure all clearances meet the approval of your local building department before installing the stove.

Providing wall and floor protection

A combustible wall or floor is one that is constructed of, or contains, a flammable material. Wood frame walls and floors covered with gypsum board, plaster, tile, cement, or other noncombustible wall covering are classified as combustible walls. Solid masonry walls and floors (unpainted brick, stone, or concrete) are considered noncombustible unless they're covered with a combustible material such as wallpaper, wood, carpet, etc.

You can reduce stove clearances to a combustible wall or floor if you first protect it with a noncombustible hearth material. Asbestos millboard has been one of the few approved materials used for reducing clearances safely. As of this writing, however, this material, along with many other products containing asbestos, is being taken off the market because it constitutes a health hazard. Appearing on the market are other insulating hearth materials that allow reduced clearances—the clearance distances will be determined both by the material and by local building codes. The drawing below shows one method approved by the NFPA for safely reducing clearances to a combustible wall and floor.

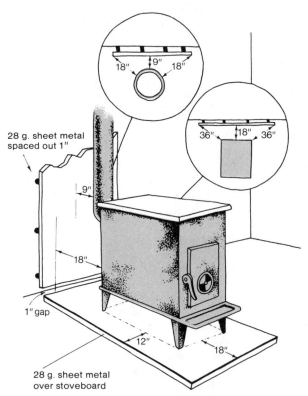

Floor and wall protection *allows reduced clearances; local codes may require still more protection.*

In addition to this protection, you must allow adequate clearance where the stovepipe enters the wall or ceiling. This is the point where the inside chimney connection joins the outside chimney. At this point, an insulated chimney support assembly or insulated pipe fitting is used to protect the

Minimum stove clearances

The following chart shows minimum space requirements between stove or stovepipe and walls, ceiling, posts, and other combustibles. It is based on standards established by the National Fire Protection Association (NFPA). The figures are intended as minimum standards and should be used only when no other specific standard is available for a particular stove. The NFPA recommends that only stoves approved by a federally certified testing laboratory be used and that these stoves be installed according to the manufacturer's clearances.

The NFPA also acknowledges "engineered systems" for protection of combustible materials. Such a system must be designed and certified by a registered professional engineer knowledgeable in heat-transfer principles. The system must also have local building department approval.

Heat source	Clearance from:			
	Top	Front	Back	Sides
Radiant stove	36"	36"	36"	36"
Circulating stove	36"	24"	12"	12"
Cookstove (unlined firebox)	30"	*	36"	36" (firing side)
				18" (opposite side)
Cookstove (lined firebox)	30"	*	24"	24" (firing side)
				18" (opposite side)
Single-wall stovepipe	18"	18"	18"	18"

Clearance to the front of a cookstove should be sufficient to permit normal use for cooking, servicing, and cleaning.

Reprinted by permission from NFPA 89M, Manual on Clearances for Heat Producing Appliances, Copyright © 1976, National Fire Protection Association, Boston, MA.

wall or ceiling (for more information on these, see "Prefabricated metal chimneys," pages 71–72).

Hearth materials and installations

Hearths for wood stoves can be made of brick, stone, tile, metal, or any other noncombustible material. A variety of attractive hearths is included in the color section starting on page 32.

Stove hearths consist of two basic sections: the floor hearth and the wall extension. Extending the hearth up the wall will not be necessary if proper clearances to combustibles are maintained, though you may wish to for purely esthetic reasons. If you wish to reduce the minimum clearances to the wall and floor safely, you must first provide the protection prescribed by your local building department before you apply the hearth materials. Masonry will transmit heat and is usually of insufficient thickness to provide adequate protection by itself. In other words, you must first install the floor and wall protection and then build the hearth over it.

Floor hearths are fairly simple to build—you just lay the bricks, tiles, or other masonry on the floor and mortar or grout the joints. If you install the prescribed floor protection, you can make an exception to the "continuous" stipulation and lay the masonry loose (no grout or mortar required)—an advantage if you want a hearth that can be moved or dismantled during the summer months.

Extending the hearth up the wall is more difficult, especially if it requires wall protection behind it— you'll need considerable experience in masonry for most of these types of installations. If you wish to attempt building a more complicated hearth, you can get help from an experienced mason or stove installer. And keep in mind that your plans must meet the approval of your local building department as a prerequisite to the installation later passing a building inspection.

Chimney & hearth location

Now that you've decided on the type of hearth you want and have determined the necessary clearances for your stove, the next step will be to determine the path the chimney and chimney connection will take. The chimney should be as vertical as possible, and avoid any obstructions, including studs, joists, or other framing members of the house. Refer to the installations pictured on page 72 to see which one best suits the intended location of your stove. In planning the location of the chimney connection (stovepipe and elbows connecting stove to outside chimney), you'll need to know the position of the stove within the location you've chosen for it. To position the stove, find out the stove's dimensions and location of its flue vent where the stovepipe is attached. If you already have the stove, and it's light enough to jockey around easily, you can set it in its intended position, allowing the proper clearances to the wall. Otherwise, make a scale drawing of the stove, its position in the room, and location of flue vent.

Next, plot out the path the chimney connection will take (see "Chimney connection," page 74). Mark the location on the wall or ceiling where the chimney connection will join the outside chimney. Here, you'll have to cut a hole through the wall or ceiling large enough to accept the chimney support assembly (ceiling supported chimneys) or insulated tee assembly (wall supported chimneys). For a discussion of these chimney components and their installation, see "Prefabricated metal chimneys" on the facing page.

Ideally, the opening in the wall or ceiling should be centered between the studs or joists, and avoid any other framing members, water pipes, electrical conduit, etc., inside the wall or ceiling. You can locate studs or joists by tapping on the wall, looking for rows of nails or tape joints, or by using a stud finder (available at hardware stores). If the support assembly or tee assembly is too large to fit between the studs or joists, you'll have to cut one of these members and frame in the correct size opening (see drawing on page 73). Before you do any cutting or drilling in the wall, mark the size of the intended hole and find its centerpoint. Then align the centerpoint of the stove's flue vent to the centerpoint of the marked opening on the wall or ceiling. Recheck stove clearances—if the stove no longer meets the required clearances once it's aligned with the chimney opening, you can either offset the chimney connection or relocate the chimney opening to provide the necessary clearance. Next, find and mark the location of the opening on the outside of the wall, or other side of ceiling. The outside location of the opening can be approximate (within an inch or two of the inside opening) because you'll be using this point to determine the run of the outside chimney. If the chimney will be running through an attic or second story, make sure there are no obstructions directly above the intended opening. You can use a plumb bob to align the ceiling opening with the intended roof opening. The chimney run should be as vertical as possible, but if you find a rafter or other framing member in the way of the chimney, you'll have to offset the pipe to avoid it. The drawing on page 72 shows an offset chimney installation. Never cut rafters—they bear the weight of the roof.

Once you know where the chimney and chimney connections will go, you can estimate the necessary materials—take all relevant information to your stove dealer or chimney supply outlet when you order them.

Once the stove is positioned, you can determine the size and location of the hearth. The hearth should provide adequate floor protection, also wall protection if the hearth continues up the wall. See pages 67 and 68 for hearth clearance requirements.

In planning hearth dimensions, it would be helpful to first draw the hearth and the location of the stove on ¼-inch graph paper (¼ inch = 1 inch), as shown in the drawing below. The graph will also come in handy for figuring hearth materials.

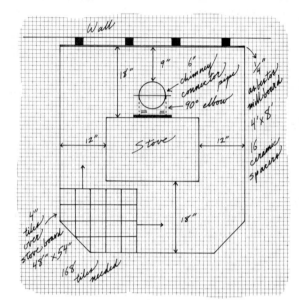

Scale drawing *on ¼-inch graph paper helps you to determine hearth size and stove position, and figure materials.*

Getting the go-ahead

Once you've planned your stove installation as accurately as possible, the next step is to submit your plans to your local building department for approval and secure a permit for installation. The building department will let you know if any additional details are required in your plan and will assign a building inspector to inspect your installation at required stages. As mentioned, you should check local building codes before you plan your stove installation. In some areas, your local fire marshal may be responsible for approving your stove and its installation for safety.

Once you have the necessary permit you can begin installing the stove. If no permit is required in your area, you should still check local building codes and follow them. Once you've installed the stove, it will have to pass building inspection. Some people attempt to "bootleg" their stove installations—that is, they don't obtain building permits or have their installations inspected by the proper authorities. Aside from getting "caught" with an illegal installation, more serious consequences may result—an unsafe stove installation can cause a house to burn down, and a homeowner's insurance won't cover the damages (see "Check on insurance," page 23). So a building permit and inspection at a cost of $10–$20 is really a bargain form of fire insurance.

Chimney installation

Three things are a *must* for a safe chimney installation: proper materials, adequate clearance, and proper assembly of all components. Faulty chimney installations cause many stove-related fires, and you should take extra care in this phase of your stove installation.

The chimney installation consists of two basic sections: the *chimney* itself (outside) and all components in the stove room making up the *chimney connection*. Installation of both sections is discussed on pages 73 and 74.

Chimney materials

Once you've determined exactly where the chimney will run, you can estimate the amount of materials you'll need. If you are planning to vent the stove into an existing chimney or flue, you need only figure the components necessary for the chimney connection (see "Using existing chimneys" on page 75).

The drawings on the next page show the standard prefabricated chimney components used in typical installations.

Chimneys for stoves may be either masonry-constructed or prefabricated metal pipe. Masonry chimneys consist of brick, concrete blocks, or stone, with special flue tile liners similar to those used for fireplaces. Professional installation of these chimneys by a mason is often prohibitive in cost, and they are difficult for the do-it-yourselfer unless you've had considerable masonry experience. It follows that prefabricated metal chimneys are most often used for new stove installations. The chimney connection usually consists of 24 gauge single wall stovepipe plus elbows and other necessary components (see "Chimney connection," page 74).

Prefabricated metal chimneys

Chimneys for wood stoves must be insulated to keep smoke and flue gases hot enough to rise up the chimney. If the flue gases cool in the chimney, the stove won't draw efficiently, and you'll get two bad results: "backpuffing" of smoke through the stove and excess creosote buildup caused by condensation of gases inside the chimney.

There are several kinds of insulated metal pipe approved for wood stove chimneys. They are listed as "Class A" (all fuel) pipe and have been tested for safety and approved by Underwriter's Laboratories, Inc. (UL). You are required to use *only* class A pipe in chimney installations. You should not make the mistake of using single wall pipe or vent pipe intended for gas or oil furnaces and water heaters.

As of this writing, there are two general types of insulated pipe suitable for wood stove insulations. Both are of multi-wall construction—one uses dead air as insulation; the other uses mineral wool, or other solid insulation. Air-insulated pipes may be of double wall or triple wall construction. Some types of triple wall pipe allow air to circulate between the pipe walls (ventilated pipe). Although defined as Class A pipe, ventilated pipe is not recommended for wood stoves because it cools the flue gases, causing excess creosote buildup.

Other components. Because houses are different and there are usually several possible locations for chimneys in any house, there are numerous prefabricated metal chimney components and fittings for different situations. Standard components for all prefabricated chimneys include insulated pipe, support assembly, roof flashing or roof jack, storm collar, and a chimney cap. Other necessary components will depend on the chimney installation.

Support assemblies include all components required to support the weight of the chimney. They're available for wall supported chimneys, roof (rafter) supported chimneys, and ceiling (joist) supported chimneys. Ceiling and roof chimney supports should be insulated or equipped with a firestop spacer so they will pass safely through combustible ceilings and roofs. Wall support assemblies include brackets and a plate that are attached to the outside wall to support the chimney. To connect a wall supported chimney to the stovepipe inside, you'll need an insulated tee so the chimney will pass safely through the wall.

Other components include wall bands (braces) to support the chimney up an outside wall, guy wires or metal braces to support the chimney above the roof, and a variety of trim and finishing collars to cover holes where the chimney passes through walls or ceilings. Common chimney installations and their components appear on the next page.

A knowledgeable stove dealer can help you choose the necessary components for your installation and provide you with everything you need. When figuring how much pipe you need for the chimney and chimney connection, always buy an extra length or two to be on the safe side. You can always return any unused lengths, provided you haven't cut them up or otherwise damaged them.

Manufacturers of prefabricated metal chimneys usually provide detailed installation instructions that will tell you how to estimate your material requirements. Remember that chimney pipe sections overlap

Common Chimney Installations

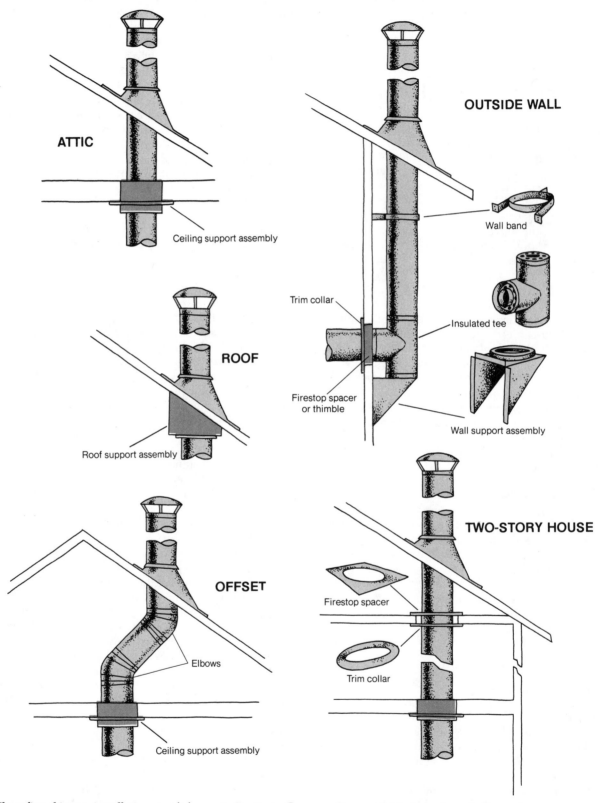

ATTIC

Ceiling support assembly

ROOF

Roof support assembly

OFFSET

Elbows

Ceiling support assembly

OUTSIDE WALL

Wall band

Trim collar

Insulated tee

Firestop spacer
or thimble

Wall support assembly

TWO-STORY HOUSE

Firestop spacer

Trim collar

These five chimney installations *work for most situations. Components—available from stove dealers and installers—may differ slightly in appearance from those pictured, depending on the manufacturer.*

when assembled, so you'll lose an inch or two from each measured pipe length.

If you're running the chimney through a second story room or finished attic, you'll need a support assembly for the first ceiling the chimney passes through and a firestop spacer for the second story ceiling and the roof. Ask your stove dealer which type of support assembly will best suit your situation. It would seem like a good idea to run single wall stovepipe through the second story room to take advantage of its radiant heat; this is bad practice if not in fact illegal. Extremely long runs of single wall pipe will cool flue gases, affecting draft and causing creosote buildup. This also applies to running single wall pipe through the wall into adjacent rooms or having extremely long horizontal runs of pipe between the stove and the chimney opening (see "Chimney connection" on page 74).

Installation tips

The following tips should be used as a general guide to help you install a prefabricated metal chimney and chimney connection. Prefabricated metal chimneys usually come with instructions for assembly and installation, or instructions are available from the manufacturer or your stove dealer. These instructions should be followed to the letter—if the chimney is not installed in strict accordance with manufacturer's instructions, your insurance company may not pay for damages resulting from a chimney fire. Because each chimney installation is slightly different, you're likely to encounter a few unique problems when you install yours. If you are having difficulty with your installation, don't hesitate to seek professional advice from a stove installer or general contractor familiar with stove installation.

Once you have all the necessary chimney components and have determined what route the chimney will take, determine where the chimney will enter the wall or ceiling (page 70) and cut a hole between the wall studs or ceiling joists for the support assembly. If the support assembly, firestop, or thimble won't fit between the studs or joists, you'll have to frame in for the parts as shown in the drawing at right. It's a good idea to turn off the electricity to the house in case you run into any wires while you're cutting.

Next, cut the outside hole and attach nailing blocks between the studs or joists to fit the support kit, thimble, or firestop spacer as shown in the drawing. If you're cutting holes in both the ceiling and roof, cut the ceiling hole first; then you can align the ceiling hole with the proposed roof hole with a plumb bob. You may have to offset the chimney pipe slightly (using two 15° or 30° elbows) to center the roof support assembly between the roof rafters or to pass pipes closer to roof ridge. Never cut roof rafters

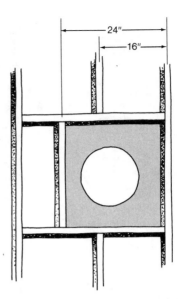

If support assembly or firestop spacer won't fit between studs or joists, frame in as shown.

under any circumstances—they support the full weight of the roof.

Pipe assembly. Once the support assembly and related fittings are installed, you are ready to install the chimney pipe sections. Before final assembly, practice fitting the pipe sections together so you get the hang of it. Insulated chimney pipe sections are interlocking: some types use slip rings to lock the sections together, others are simply fitted together and twisted 1/8 turn to lock them in position. Each section is marked with an arrow, or the word "UP," so you don't install the sections upside down.

The first section of pipe is fitted into the support assembly. Once the first section is installed securely, attach any collars, flashings, etc., by slipping them over the pipe into position before attaching additional lengths of pipe.

Above the roof. Once the chimney pipe is installed up to the roof level, you're ready to install the final components. The drawing on the next page shows a typical roof installation. Because this section of the chimney is exposed to the elements, you'll need flashing (adjustable to the roof pitch) and a storm collar to seal the opening around the pipe. The flashing slips over the first section of pipe above the roof line, is nailed in place, and its edges sealed against the roof with roofing cement (available at hardware stores). Next, the storm collar is fitted over the flashing (as shown in the drawing) and tightened to the pipe with a screw clamp.

In order for the chimney to draw properly, it should extend at least 3 feet above the point it exits the roof and 2 feet higher than any point of the roof

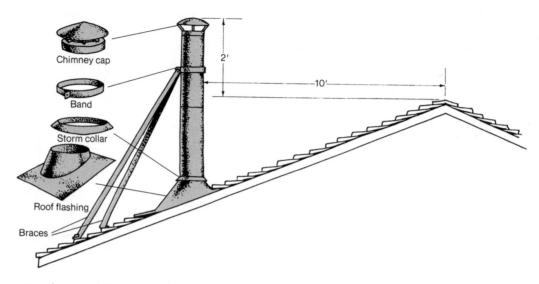

Chimney section *above roof line must extend at least 3 feet above roof opening, 2 feet above highest point within 10 feet. Chimneys extending 5 feet or more above roof require bracing.*

within 10 feet on a horizontal plane (see drawing above). If the chimney is 5 feet or more above the roof opening, it will require bracing. You can use either guy wires or metal chimney braces for this purpose. You can get chimney braces from your stove dealer or make them from ¾ inch metal electrical conduit.

Wall installations. If you run the chimney pipe up an exterior wall, you'll probably have to contend with a roof overhang. If the overhang is only a few inches, such as a fascia board on the gable end of a roof, you can attach spacer blocks between the wall and the mounting brackets that hold the pipe. If the overhang or eaves extend less than 4 inches beyond the center of the pipe, you can use two 15° elbows on the chimney to clear them. If the eaves project past this point, you will have to install the standard roof support assembly. Two of these situations are shown in the drawing at right.

The insulated tee used to connect the chimney pipe to the inside stovepipe should pass completely through the wall and end flush with inside wall surface. If the tee is too short, obtain a short insulated extension from your stove dealer.

Topping off the chimney. The final component of your outside chimney installation is the chimney cap or chimney topper. There are several types available —all are designed to keep water, snow, and animals out of the chimney; some have wire mesh spark arresters to keep sparks and burning material from escaping out the top of the chimney. If heavy winds are a problem in your area, you may need a special rotating cap that keeps the flue opening out of the wind.

Chimney connection

Pipe used to connect the stove to the chimney opening is 24 gauge, single wall black stovepipe. You should not use lighter gauge pipe such as galvanized pipe used for venting gas and oil furnaces. Lighter gauge pipe will disintegrate quickly if used with a wood-burning appliance and is downright dangerous should you have a chimney fire.

Stovepipe comes in 6–7–8 inch diameters to fit all American stoves. On many European stoves, the flue collar that connects to the pipe has a slightly larger

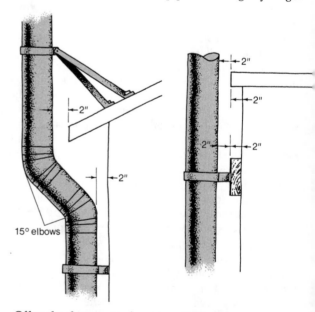

Offset the chimney *to clear eaves (left), or use spacers the width of overhang (right). If eaves extend 4 inches past pipe's center, install as shown on page 72.*

or smaller diameter than the standard 6–7–8 inch pipe (Europeans use metric sizes). If you have one of these stoves, you'll need a flue adapter ring to attach the stovepipe to the stove's flue collar (available at stove dealers who carry European stoves). If possible, the diameter of the stovepipe should be the same size or only slightly larger than the flue opening in the stove. Reducing the opening will most likely result in a poor chimney draft, causing smoke to backpuff from the stove.

Depending on the location of your stove and the chimney opening in the wall or ceiling, you may need one or more elbows for the stovepipe connection. Most installations require only one or two 90° elbows. If your flue connection requires a bend less than 90°, you can buy an adjustable elbow which will make bends from 0° to 90°. Some stoves, including most of the older nonairtight ones, may require the use of a flue damper to control the draft (see "Anatomy of a stove" on page 10). Should your stove require one, you should install it in the first section of the stovepipe 6–12 inches above the flue collar of the stove.

Draft. Modern airtight stoves are usually so efficient at radiating heat that their flue temperatures are usually lower than nonairtight stoves, especially when they're damped down to a slow burn. If flue temperatures in the chimney are too low, the smoke and gases will slow down, restricting draft. Single wall stovepipe will radiate additional heat, causing the flue gases to cool even further. For this reason, the chimney connection for airtight stoves should be as short and direct as possible—a straight vertical run of pipe from the stove to the ceiling or a short horizontal run of pipe from the back of the stove to a chimney opening directly behind it. On nonairtight stoves, or stoves that create high flue temperatures, longer runs of single wall pipe in the room will increase heat output in the room. Keep in mind that long runs of pipe collect more creosote than short runs and will have to be cleaned more often. Heating efficiency of these stoves can be improved by installation of a heat recovery device in the stove or stovepipe above the stove (see "Heat recovery devices" on page 21). Your stove dealer or an installer familiar with your brand of stove can advise you on the proper length for your flue connection. Draft will be restricted by bends in the stovepipe. It's difficult to specify just how many bends in the chimney connection you can get away with because draft is affected by so many other variables—length and height of outside chimney, local weather conditions, the stove and how it's operated, etc. The average chimney connection usually has no more than two 90° bends, and this seems to be a good rule of thumb in most cases.

Assembly tips. Stovepipe generally has one crimped end with a slightly smaller diameter so the pipes will fit together. Stovepipe sections are assembled crimped ends down so creosote won't leak through the pipe joints. You may have to trim off the crimped end of the first section so the pipe will fit the flue collar on your stove. Sections are fastened together with three sheet metal screws. Both horizontal and vertical runs of pipe longer than 6 feet should have external support. Hangers and wall braces for this purpose are available from your stove dealer. Be sure all pipe and fittings have the required 18-inch clearance from combustible surfaces (see "Stove and stovepipe clearances" on page 67). If your chimney connection requires a long run of horizontal pipe (4 feet or more) the pipe should slope upward from the stove to the chimney opening at least ¼ inch per foot of run. If you need to cut any lengths of pipe, a pair of heavy tin snips, hacksaw, or portable jigsaw with a metal cutting blade can be used (when using the jigsaw, you'll have to start the cut with a hacksaw). Be careful not to bend the pipe out of shape when cutting. Some prefabricated chimney manufacturers have flue connection kits which include enough interlocking pipe and necessary components to do a single installation.

The final length of stovepipe connects to the chimney support assembly or insulated chimney fitting in the wall or ceiling. *Never* run single wall pipe into or through a combustible wall.

Using existing chimneys

Many older homes have unused masonry chimneys or flues that were blocked off when the original coal, gas, or wood stove was removed. The inside chimney opening was usually covered with a metal disk to prevent drafts from entering the room. If your house has an existing but unused chimney (never vent more than one heating device into the same flue) you may be able to use it for your stove. However, the chimney must meet four requirements:

1) It must be in good repair.

2) It must have a fireclay liner at least ⅝ inch thick.

3) The chimney opening in the room (thimble) and the chimney's inside flue diameter must be the same size or larger than the diameter of the stove's flue connection (stovepipe).

4) The metal or fireclay thimble leading into the flue must meet local codes and provide adequate clearance for wood stove installations (see page 67). If the chimney opening does not have a thimble, or the thimble is the wrong size, you'll have to install one.

Have the chimney checked thoroughly by a professional mason, chimney sweep, or the local fire department. In older chimneys, the fireclay liners can develop cracks, and mortar between the bricks or the liner can deteriorate. Leaky chimneys cause fires. If the chimney needs repairs, first get an estimate from a mason. You may find it will cost more to repair the old chimney than to install a new one. If the chimney needs cleaning, have it cleaned before you hook up the stove.

Venting into the fireplace

Another way to save the cost of installing a new chimney is to connect the stove to an existing fireplace. The chimney should be clean and in good repair; also, the fireplace should draw properly. If you vent a stove into a smoky, inefficient fireplace, you'll most likely have a smoky, inefficient stove installation.

Some stoves are made to fit inside the fireplace opening (these are discussed on page 10). With all other stoves, though, you'll have to block off the fireplace opening and vent the stove into it. The drawings at right show two common ways to do it. Other installations appear in color photographs on pages 60 and 61. Once you've decided which way you'll be venting the stove, check with your building department to be sure the installation will meet local codes.

Most fireplace hearths are not wide enough to provide the necessary clearances from the stove to a combustible floor in front of the hearth. If this is true of yours, you'll have to provide adequate floor protection as described on page 68 or extend the hearth to meet the clearance requirement.

There are two factors that may contribute to poor draft once the stove is vented into the fireplace. First, the size of the stove must be in proportion to that of the flue into which it is vented. If a tiny stove is vented into a very large fireplace chimney, the temperature may be too low and the volume of flue gases leaving the stove may be insufficient to assure proper draft. An experienced stove dealer will be able to recommend the correct stove size for your fireplace chimney.

The other draft-restricting factor is a too-short chimney. If you find after you've made the stove connection that the chimney doesn't draw properly, you can extend the height by adding one or two sections of prefabricated metal chimney to the masonry one. To do this, you'll need the required amount of pipe, a starter or anchor plate for mounting the first section of pipe, chimney braces if the extension is high enough to require them, and a chimney cap. Components for prefabricated metal chimneys are discussed on page 71.

Some fireplaces are constructed with multiple flues, one of them unused, intended for future additions such as the stove you just bought. If your fireplace has one of these, you're lucky because you'll be able to use both fireplace and stove. Make sure it is unused, though, and not already used to vent gas or oil furnaces, ovens, or other heating devices. It will be helpful to have a mason find the

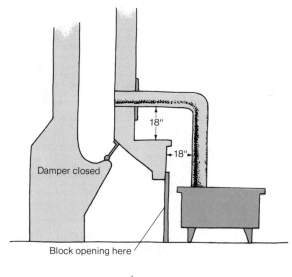

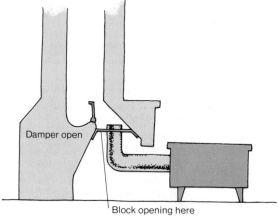

These two methods *of venting a stove into a fireplace meet most local codes. First method (top) works best for top-vented stove; second method for back-vented stoves. Masonry or metal blocks opening behind stove (top); sheet metal blocks opening below damper (bottom).*

exact location of the flue for you and determine the best spot to vent the stove. Breaking into a masonry chimney can be tricky work, especially if the chimney is covered by a stud wall, so you'll probably want the work done by a professional.

Because most stoves tend to produce more soot and creosote than fireplaces do, the chimney will have to be cleaned and inspected more frequently.

The final inspection

Once your stove is connected to the chimney and the installation is complete, go back and check the entire chimney and chimney connection, inch by inch. Make sure all joints and other components are fastened securely. Next, light a small smoky fire (damp leaves or newspaper work well) in the stove, then check the chimney again for smoke leaks. Make any final repairs necessary—then you're ready to use your stove.

Build it from a barrel

Barrel stove kits provide a practical means of heating large spaces—workshops, basements, rustic cabins, and the like. What they lack in beauty they make up in economy—and they produce a tremendous amount of heat.

Kits range in price from about $25 to $70. Most include cast-iron door, flue collar, legs, and all hardware needed for assembly—everything's there but the barrel. You can purchase a drum from most wholesale oil distributors. The barrel is likely to burn out within a few years, but the fittings are easily transferred to a new barrel. Here's how to proceed.

1. Gather *all stove parts and accompanying hardware and note correct relationships.*

2. Center *stove door assembly on barrel, open door, and mark its inside perimeter on barrel. Do the same for flue collar.*

3. Drill *starter holes through each scribe line and cut out door and flue openings with metal-cutting saber saw.*

4. Recenter *door assembly and collar over openings; mark and drill bolt holes.*

5. Bolt *door and collar to barrel, using bolts and nuts provided with kit.*

6. Place *stove on legs and maneuver it until door is level. Mark, drill, and bolt one set of legs.*

7. Invert *barrel and place a board across both set of legs. When board rests evenly, drill and bolt second set of legs.*

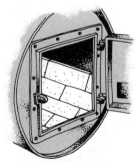

8. Line *inside of finished stove with firebrick or a 3 to 4-inch layer of sand to protect firebox.*

9. Stove *is now ready for installation —see "Installing your stove," page 66.*

Using Your Stove

Most long-time wood stove users agree that the cozy radiant heat of their stoves more than repays the effort that goes into producing it—but it does require effort. Wood stoves are not automatic appliances; they require a break-in period—both of stove and stove owner. Here are some pointers to start you off in the right direction.

Firing the stove

Safety, fire management, ash removal, and maintenance are largely matters of common sense and experience and are not difficult to master. Invest a little time in learning about the care and feeding of your stove, and it will repay you many times over. Here's how to begin.

Safety first!

The operation of a wood stove can be quite safe and convenient, but its very convenience can lead you to relax your vigilance. You should never lose sight of the fact that there is a box with a fire in it in your house. Some tips for safe operation:
• Burn only well-seasoned hardwoods. Softwood is best for kindling, not for fuel—it's too smoky, makes sparks, and its resins form creosote much faster than hardwoods do. Never burn green wood of any kind.
• Never leave the fire unattended. Sparks can escape from open draft inlets. If you must hold a fire overnight, be sure the drafts are turned down. It's best to have only glowing embers in the stove when you retire for the evening.
• *Never* use any sort of flammable liquid to start or encourage the fire—not even charcoal lighter. Use of

these liquids in the enclosed firebox of a stove can produce an explosion.
• Keep combustibles at least three feet away from the stove. It's easy to misjudge the power of radiated heat, since it doesn't heat the air. A hot stove is a remarkably effective fire starter when combustibles are too close.
• Exercise extreme caution any time the door is open —embers may still be present and can pop out even when the fire appears to be dead.
• Never burn trash in your stove. The fast, hot fire will abuse the stove and flue. For the same reason, sawdust logs and chemical logs should never be used —they burn too hot.

Building the fire

Once your stove is installed you should make a small test fire; the idea is to create enough smoke to check the tightness of all seams and connections without committing yourself to an hours-long blaze. The test fire can be nothing more than a few sheets of newspaper, perhaps with some wet leaves to insure enough smoke. Be sure all dampers are open before you light the fire, and be sure you have followed all manufacturer's instructions for preparing the stove. Once your installation checks out, you are ready to begin in earnest.

Most stoves need to be broken in or "seasoned." To do this, make the first few fires small and avoid sudden bursts of heat. At first, condensation will tend to occur on the stove, and this should be wiped away continuously so it does not stain the surface. If your stove is painted, it may "smell funny" at first; this is only the oil in the paint evaporating—it will stop after the first few fires.

Fire building *varies according to your stove's draft pattern. For an updraft stove (left), place kindling under logs and light fire; S-draft stove (center) should be kindled only in front. Downdraft stove (right) needs an "upside-down" fire, since it burns from top to bottom.*

To build a fire, crumple newspaper sheets into balls and distribute them over the bottom of the fire box; follow these with dry kindling—preferably split, dry softwood such as lumber scraps, about ½–1 inch in diameter. Allowing air passages between the sticks, lay the kindling in a crisscross fashion, but make sure the sticks are close enough together to allow fire to spread from one to the other.

Follow this kindling layer with several pieces of dry, seasoned hardwood, progressing from smaller to larger pieces. Again, arrange these so that air can circulate around them, but close enough to "feed" each other once they're burning. Don't forget that a fire needs heat, oxygen, and fuel to burn: packing kindling too tightly will exclude oxygen from the fire. In fact, this is probably the most common cause of failure in fire building.

Two exceptions to this fire-laying procedure are downdraft and S-draft stoves (see page 11 for a description of these stoves). The fire-laying procedure is reversed in a downdrafter—start with the larger logs and progress to light kindling and newspaper. Scandinavian stoves and other S-draft stoves need only the front ends of the logs kindled; kindling is not needed over the whole bottom of the firebox.

Once the fire is laid, check that the flue damper is open and that the stove draft controls are set for maximum draft. Light the newspaper and immediately close the door. Don't be tempted to have a look to see the logs start burning; they'll do much better with the regulated draft provided by the stove's controls than they will with the excess air flowing through the open door.

If your first attempt fails, try again with fresh kindling and paper. If your kindling is dry, patience and persistence will be rewarded. In fact, once you've learned your stove's fire-starting idiosyncrasies, you'll probably find it easier to light than a fireplace or campfire.

Managing the fire

Trial and error will be your guides once the fire is burning. Stoves differ in the amount of fuel they need, and the size of your house and rate of firing will have an effect on your fire.

Temperature control. The heat output of your stove is governed by the size of the fire, which is in turn governed by the damper and air inlet settings as well as the amount of fuel in the firebox. Generally, the more air passing through the stove, the hotter the fire will burn—as long as it is supplied with fuel. To slow the fire, turn down the inlet drafts, the damper, or both. Better yet, refrain from overstoking the firebox.

A common complaint—or boast—of wood stove owners is that their stoves "drive them out of the house" with heat. This can be prevented by first of all choosing a stove with the correct heating capacity for your situation. (See "Heating capacity," page 19.) The relatively small size of most stoves is deceptive; most are quite powerful if fired at their maximum rate. Yet, this is what you should try to do, at least part of the time, to keep the flue clean. Strive to regulate the heat output of your stove by adjusting the amount of fuel you add, not by constantly damping down the fire. If your stove is not oversized for your situation, this should be possible.

Reloading. When you reload your stove, it is a good idea to open the draft controls and damper before opening the door. This will help prevent backpuffing of smoke into the room. Also, wait until the chimney is warm and the draft well established before you refuel the stove.

After reloading, run the stove with dampers and inlets open for about half an hour; this will help retard the formation of creosote, most of which is given off in the early stages of firing (see next page for more on creosote). The best time to damp down your stove is after the fire has reached the coaling stage and most of the wood has been consumed.

Banking the fire. To make fire starting easier each day, bank your fire the previous night by raking the last of the evening's coals and embers into the center of the stove. Cover them with ashes and close the draft controls to minimum setting. A thick layer of ashes will exclude most air from the coals and prevent their burning up during the night. Uncover them in the morning, rake them to the front of the stove, and place several pieces of firewood on top. Close the door, open the drafts all the way, and in a few minutes your morning's fire will be burning.

Ash layer, *insulating coals and keeping out excess air, allows coals to burn all night. Banking the fire in this manner keeps the stove warm and makes it easy to start the fire the next day.*

Overnight burning. It is here that you are likely to run into a contradiction between good practice in stove operation and the claims of manufacturers. While stove companies are fond of advertising how long their products will hold a fire, long burns on a single load of fuel are inefficient and promote the formation of creosote and soot. It is better to load the stove more frequently with less wood and burn it hotter; this requires more labor, but it maintains a cleaner flue and is safer.

If there is a real need to hold a fire, not just glowing coals, overnight, most airtight stoves can do it. Place one or two large logs on a good bed of coals, operate the stove at full draft until the wood is well-ignited, then turn down the inlet draft controls to minimum setting. The moisture and tars driven off

by this low, smoldering fire will produce creosote during the night, but you can burn off much of the fresh creosote by running a hot fire the next morning provided your chimney is not already laden with deposits. In general, you should avoid overnight fires if at all possible.

Stove & flue maintenance

Regular attention paid to your stove and flue will pay you back in increased satisfaction and in the security of knowing your wood heating system is safe. Most stoves need little maintenance; beyond a regular cleaning, neither does a quality chimney installation. Properly maintained, a wood stove will last for many years—or even generations.

Ashes, ashes

If you are a novice at using an airtight stove, you are in for a pleasant surprise. Because of their efficient burning characteristics, these stoves accumulate only small amounts of ash, compared to nonairtight types. Eventually, of course, ashes will build up in every stove and have to be removed.

Stoves with built-in ash pans need not be emptied until the pan is full; in fact, a layer of ashes in any stove will help encourage the fire—it acts as an insulator, holding the heat in the coals at the bottom of the fire. For ash removal, you should have a fireproof, covered container into which you can shovel the ashes. Avoid using a broom, except for touch-ups; vigorous sweeping will only send a cloud of ash through the room. Be sure to leave the container outdoors in a safe place until you are quite certain there are no more embers; only then should the ashes finally be disposed of.

Antique coal scuttle *looks good on the hearth and provides a safe and convenient means of removing ashes.*

But don't overlook the possibility of using your ashes. Ash is simply wood minus its water and carbon compounds; what remains is rich in minerals and has many uses in the garden as a nutrient, soil conditioner, or even as a pest repellent.

Creosote

Creosote is formed when moisture expelled from burning wood combines with combustible gases escaping unburned up the flue. This messy, tarry substance is an almost unavoidable byproduct of wood combustion, and one of the stove owner's biggest problems.

If layers of creosote build up on the flue lining, the draft will be restricted and the black, tarry creosote will bake on and become brittle and shiny. This deposit is highly flammable; if not removed regularly, a chimney fire may result.

How it is formed. Paradoxically, airtight stoves—preferable for efficient heating—tend to make more creosote than do open fireplaces and nonairtight stoves. Stoves and fireplaces sending a lot of heat up their flues will not make much creosote because their flue temperatures are likely to be too high for creosote deposits to form, even if creosote is present in the flue gases. But airtight stoves that are repeatedly burned at low draft settings (which cause low flue temperatures and incomplete combustion) will quickly build up creosote deposits.

Stoves that have good secondary air systems and are fired near their capacity will have substantially fewer problems with creosote. The combustible gases are burned away during secondary combustion, and those gases that do enter the flue are carried away by the strong, hot draft.

Creosote collects most heavily in the coolest portions of the flue; in most installations, this will be near the top of the chimney. Metal chimneys may have fewer problems than masonry types since their relatively higher rate of thermal expansion and contraction tends to fracture creosote deposits. This causes the deposits to flake away and fall back into the fire.

What you can do about it. To avoid excess creosote, you must sacrifice some stove efficiency: this is the essential paradox in using wood heat. If the flue temperature falls much below 300°F/149°C, creosote deposits will begin to form. So you must send some of your hard-earned heat up the flue to prevent this from happening. Just how much will depend upon your stove. Thermometers that attach to the flue pipe are available to help you monitor flue temperatures.

Many stoves have secondary combustion systems that introduce hot air at a location just above or beyond the primary combustion zone. The hot gases, ideally, ignite when mixed with this secondary air. It is difficult to maintain the necessary hot temperatures, however, except during the hottest part of the firing cycle, so it is unlikely that complete secondary combustion will take place throughout the firing cycle in most stoves.

True, a hot fire and good secondary combustion are helpful in avoiding creosote formation, but regular cleaning of your chimney will prove your strongest ally. Inspect your chimney and connecting pipes regularly. Plan to clean the flue at least once a year, more often if the stove is in daily use—especially if you burn it overnight at low settings. Creosote is part of wood heating, but it need not be a hazard.

Chimney & flue

You don't need the top hat of a traditional chimney sweep, but you do need his steel brush. Responsible operation of a wood stove calls for regular chimney inspection and at least yearly cleaning. The importance of this cannot be overstressed.

Modern-day chimney sweep, *reviving the trade, often adopts traditional garb. Check your Yellow Pages under "Chimney Cleaning" to find a chimney sweep near you.*

The job is messy, but not intimidating unless your chimney is very long or your roof is steeply pitched. In these cases you should hire a professional sweep. Along with the wood stove, sweeps are coming back from an earlier era, and often they bring the hat along with the brush.

If you elect to do the job yourself, here are a few tips:

• Use a brush. Don't use chains, bags of rocks, or other heavy implements; these will damage your flue

Chimney-sweeping brushes *are available in a wide range of shapes and sizes. Your dealer can help you choose.*

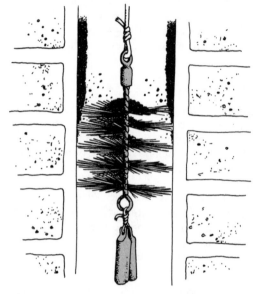

Upward movement *of brush scrapes off creosote accumulation; window sash weights pull the brush down again after each pass up the flue.*

and aren't as effective as a good steel brush.

• Use masking tape and newspaper to cover any openings, and to cover nearby furniture.

• Use a dust mask for eyes and mouth.

To clean the flue, attach the brush to a rope the length of your chimney. Attach weights, such as window sash weights, to the end of the brush. Pass the brush down to the bottom of the flue and pull it up again. This operation should be repeated a half-dozen times or until the brush no longer brings up large amounts of creosote and soot.

For long horizontal runs of pipe, fiberglass rods are available that attach to the brush and allow you to push it through. These are also useful if you must clean your flue from below, as may be the case if your roof is too steep for safety.

A heavy-duty vacuum is useful for cleaning out the hearth or stove; but don't use your household vacuum—the ashes will ruin its motor. Clean your stovepipe sections by dismantling them, carrying them outside, and cleaning them with the brush.

Finally, check your flue thoroughly with a flashlight to be really sure it's clean, and then reassemble your stovepipe. Now, assured of comfort and safety, you're ready for another heating season.

Stove upkeep

The need for maintenance increases in proportion to stove use. If yours is a hard worker, one that is fired daily through the heating season, plan to check it at

least once a year. Then it will go on working hard for you in years to come.

Surface. To maintain a painted surface, a yearly retouching with a high-temperature paint or stove polish is necessary. This prevents rusting and hides the "chalking" that occurs on most matte-surfaced stoves. Porcelain enamel surfaces, although delicate and somewhat expensive, need only an occasional wiping with a damp sponge.

Firebox. Check the grates and burn plates, if any, for burnout. These parts are subject to considerable heat stress and will eventually become oxidized and need replacement. Be sure the firebox is adequately protected by sand or ashes if it has no grate.

Doors. The gaskets used to seal the doors on most airtight stoves will need replacement every few years. Your dealer should be able to supply you with new ones.

Seams. Iron stoves with seams sealed by furnace cement should be carefully checked. The cement eventually dries out and becomes brittle. Unless seams are very tight, the cement may eventually fall out. Fresh cement is available at most dealers and is easily applied.

As we've said, stove maintenance is rather like keeping your car in shape. Properly looked after, your stove—like your car—will give you many years of service and may never need an overhaul.

A Woodchopper's Guide

Heating with wood, unlike most conventional heating methods, most often requires that you seek out and transport your own fuel supply, as you would your groceries. First, you must decide which wood species in your area make the best fuelwoods, then you have to locate a source for them. After you've done this, it's just a matter of getting the wood from the source to the stove. This guide will help you choose the best fuelwoods, find them, bring them home, and prepare them—cut, stacked, and seasoned—to feed the stove.

Which woods burn best?

All wood is divided into two general categories—hardwoods and softwoods. Hardwoods include all species of broad-leafed, usually deciduous, trees (i.e. oak, hickory, maple). Softwoods include the conifers and other needleleaf evergreens (pine, fir, cedar). Pound for pound, all woods have about the same heating value. By volume, though, the denser hardwoods generally have a higher heat value than softwoods. A cord of hickory, for example, has about twice the heat value of a cord of pine, all other things being equal. Refer to the chart on page 7 for a more complete comparison of the heat values of common fuelwoods.

Because hardwoods are generally denser and less resinous than softwoods, they burn more slowly, producing a more even heat. Softwoods burn hot and fast, making them excellent for kindling, but if you use them as your primary fuel, you'll be feeding the stove more frequently and going through wood as you would a pair of two-dollar shoes. Because of their high resin (sap) content, softwoods also produce more creosote than hardwoods, which means more frequent flue cleaning.

Heat values aside, wood species within the two major categories have individual characteristics that may or may not make them choice fuelwood. For instance, straight grained woods—such as birch or red oak—are easier to split than woods with spiral or intertwined grain patterns. Ironwood or hardhack has well earned its appellations, if you can judge by the saw blades and ax bits dulled in its cutting. Some woods, including many softwoods, are heavy smoke producers; others contain moisture pockets which cause them to snap, crackle, and pop, throwing off sparks as they burn—a consideration when you're burning wood in open stoves and fireplaces. Many fruitwoods, apple being the most popular, burn with a pleasant fragrance.

Most oldtimers and experienced wood burners in your area will obligingly praise, damn, or offer advice on the burning qualities of indigenous woods. They will probably agree that among the best fuelwoods, overall, are ash, beech, birch, hickory, oak (all species), and hard maple. They have high heat values, burn well, produce little smoke, and split fairly easily.

Seasoned wood

Wood should be well-seasoned before it's burned. Over half the total weight of green or freshly cut wood is water. Air-drying or seasoning wood reduces its moisture content substantially, thereby increasing its heat value. Aside from rendering up to 20 percent more heat, seasoned wood weighs less, so it's easier to handle and transport than green wood. It also ignites more quickly, burns better, and produces less smoke and creosote than green wood.

When buying wood, there's no absolute way to tell if it's fully seasoned, but you can get a rough idea if it's seasoned enough for burning by knocking two pieces of wood together. A resonant cracking—like the sound of a baseball bat hitting a hardball—in-dicates the pieces are relatively dry. A dull thud indi-cates the wood is still green. Large cracks in the ends of the pieces are also an indication of seasoned wood. Relative weights of green and dry wood are another indication, if you have two equal-sized pieces for comparison. For tips on how to season wood, see page 87.

Locating your source

Unless you're fortunate enough to have a woodlot or section of forest on your property, you'll have to lo-cate one or more reliable sources for your fuelwood. If you opt to buy wood, you need not look any far-ther than your phone book or the classified ads in your local newspaper. If, however, you're somewhat more ambitious, you may want to seek out sources of wood free for the taking. If you choose the latter course, you'll have to invest in some wood cutting tools, figure in transportation costs, and resign your-self to working up a sweat getting the wood from its source to your stove. To paraphrase an old line, there ain't no such thing as a free woodpile.

Buying wood

If you find scavenging for wood impractical for you, then it's to your advantage to become a smart wood shopper. Once you're familiar with the best fuelwoods in your area and can tell if they're seasoned properly, learn how to tell if you're getting a full measure for the price you pay.

Measures. Wood is measured by the cord, a term so familiar that nearly all of us presume we know what it means. Experienced wood burners, however, know that a "cord" may represent more than one measure-ment.

A *standard cord* is a pile of wood 4 feet high by 4 feet wide by 8 feet long. This equals 128 cubic feet—80 cubic feet of solid wood, 48 cubic feet of air space between the pieces. The standard cord you buy may contain more or less wood than the above, depending on how the wood is stacked, so you should learn to develop an eye for tight stacking.

A *face cord* measures 4 feet high by 8 feet long, but less than 4 feet wide. A face cord 2 feet wide, then, would equal only half a standard cord; a face cord 16 inches wide would equal only a third of a standard cord. Whether called a face cord, run, or rick, its price should reflect its relationship to a standard cord.

Another popular way of selling wood is by the truckload. The volume of wood, of course, is deter-mined by how much wood is loaded in the truck. The only way to know the true measure is either to load your own truck, or ask the dealer what percentage of

a cord he's loading on his truck and hope he's honest.

Remember too, that if you're having your wood delivered, you'll probably be paying a bit extra for it, and you may not get a chance to measure the amount until after it's piled on your doorstep. And one addi-tional reminder: if you want to avoid extra work, be sure to buy wood that fits into your stove.

Finding wood

There's a variety of potential sources for free, or almost free, firewood. The quality of these woods will vary from softwood kindling (such as lumber scraps from construction sites) to good-sized hardwood logs. If you live in an urban area, your sources may be limited; but even downtown residents in major cities have a few options, as you will note in the sugges-tions below.

If you plan to become a serious wood scavenger, you'll need a truck or trailer capable of transporting a good-sized load of wood, especially if you have to travel any distance to get it. You'll also need tools; a chainsaw, ax, and other cutting and splitting tools are musts and will pay for themselves after a few seasons of steady woodburning. These tools are shown in the drawing on page 87.

The following suggestions are not a complete list, but only a thought-provoking sampler of possible sources for free, or practically free, wood.

Construction sites. Building construction, remodel-ing, or demolition always leave some scrap—mostly short bits of dimensional lumber, usually pine and fir. In most cases, the contractor or foreman will let you remove some of the trash—but ask first. Failure to ask permission may result in prosecution for theft, as the contractor may have prearranged trash re-moval and salvage agreements.

Garbage dumps. Here, you're most likely to find trimmings, packing crates, and bits of lumber from remodeling jobs. Most dump proprietors and waste haulers salvage from their own sites and thus forbid scavenging, but you may be able to work out an arrangement with the proprietor or whoever's in charge to allow you to remove wood.

Parks. Park maintenance includes trimming trees and felling dead or diseased trees. A check with the local department of parks may turn up more than one source of wood. This is one of the best opportunities for city dwellers to obtain choice hardwoods for burning, though the wood will most likely require seasoning.

Utility companies. Electric and telephone rights of way require constant maintenance. Utility crews trim branches regularly to keep them from interfering with wires, and often the wood is available for the taking. Call your local utilities' offices for permission and information on current work sites.

Large landholders. Many farmers and ranchers have more downed wood than they can use themselves. Sometimes they must remove trees to accommodate expanded plantings; other times, they have to thin orchards of dead trees or remove them entirely. So they may welcome your offer to remove wood. Timber companies are another possibility. They usually leave a good deal of unmerchantable timber on their property after a logging operation. Keeping an ear to the ground and seeking advice from knowledgeable locals, combined with inquiry into large land ownerships, will keep you abreast of the wood gathering possibilities in your area.

State and national forests. Forest conservation requires periodic thinning of dead and diseased trees and removal of downed wood. Most state and national forestry services have programs that allow wood removal by private individuals. If you are fortunate enough to live within the vicinity of a state or national forest, contact your local forestry service for details on designated wood removal areas. You'll most likely have to secure a permit and perhaps pay a token fee for the wood you take.

From tree to stove

If you're harvesting your own firewood, your best bet is to go after dead or downed wood. Felling a standing tree over 15 feet or so is tricky and dangerous work. The skill involved can't be learned from this or any other book. If, however, your wood source is standing trees, always work with a seasoned veteran when felling them, or hire an insured professional tree cutter to do the work. To find a professional, look in the Yellow Pages of the phone book under "Tree Service."

The rest of the work—limbing, bucking, and splitting—is well within the capability of most novices, provided certain safety measures are taken. Along with the usual assortment of woodcutting tools (see drawing on page 87), a hardhat, safety goggles, heavy gloves, and a sturdy pair of boots are standard equipment for working with downed trees. The following sequence of steps will guide you in turning a downed tree into stove-sized pieces of firewood.

Limbing

The first step in cutting a downed tree is to cut off its limbs flush with the trunk. A chain saw or hand-saw and an ax are standard tools for limbing. The saw is for larger limbs, the ax for smaller ones (see drawing on page 87).

Cautions. Chain saws are dangerous; their misuse, especially on downed trees, can cause serious injury. Novices should work under the supervision of an experienced operator until thoroughly familiar with the saw and the job it's doing. Even those experienced with chain saws should work with a partner whenever they use one—accidents do happen.

Before doing any cutting, though, study the downed tree to determine which of its limbs support the weight of the tree on the ground. These supporting limbs are under extreme pressure and should not be cut until the free limbs have been removed to lessen the tension on them. If you cut the supporting limbs first, they can whip out at you unexpectedly or cause the tree to shift, resulting in a serious, even fatal, injury.

Free branches. When you start removing the free limbs (those not supporting the tree), work from the base of the trunk toward the top. Make all cuts as flush to the trunk as possible. (Stubs protruding from the trunk can lead to accidents when you're bucking the trunk and handling the pieces.) Try, as much as possible, to stand on the side of the trunk opposite the branch you're cutting in order to have the trunk as a shield between you and the ax or saw. Remember, though, if you're using a chain saw, you'll have to keep it close to and in front of you to maintain control over it—never hold it at arm's length or out to one side when cutting. Keeping the limb between you and the saw, or ax, cut limbs from the base side to the crotch (see drawing below).

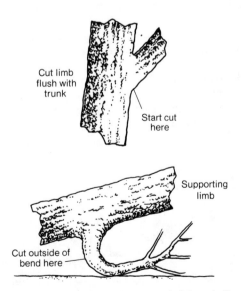

Cut limb flush with trunk

Start cut here

Supporting limb

Cut outside of bend here

Cut *free limbs from base side to crotch (above). Cut supporting limbs on outside of bend (below).*

Supporting branches. While you're removing the free branches, you'll also be cutting some of the supporting branches as you cut your way up the trunk. Leave a few of these branches to support the trunk—this will make bucking easier when the time comes. The supporting branches will be bent under pressure from the weight of the trunk, so cut them on the outside curve of the bend. If you cut on the inside curve, the pressure on the limb will close the saw kerf (or cut), binding the saw (see drawing on page 85). It's always wise to have an ax or second saw handy: a second cut farther from the trunk will release a bound tool.

Bucking

Cutting (bucking) the trunk and major branches into stove-length sections can be done with either a chain saw or a hand saw. First, measure each length, then mark by scoring with a light saw cut. Working from the tip of the trunk to the base, cut the trunk into sections as marked, and cut the supporting branches as you get to them.

Some lengths will be supported directly by a branch, free lengths will not, and the techniques for bucking them will differ. If a section is free (not supported directly by a branch), first make an undercut one-third the thickness of the section, then finish the cut from the topside. This allows the section to drop straight down. Cutting completely through the section from the top side often causes the outer end to drop first. Should this happen, the section could swing inward and rap a leg or foot.

If a section is supported by a branch, reverse the procedure. Make the first cut from the top, one-third through the thickness of the section, then finish with an undercut. Cutting a supported section completely through the top can cause the supported piece to buckle inward, binding the saw. The same pressure tends to open a bottom cut. (Techniques for cutting free and supported lengths are illustrated in the drawing below.)

If the trunk rests directly on the ground, make all cuts halfway through the thickness of the tree. Then, using a peavey (see drawing on facing page), roll the trunk over and finish all cuts from the opposite side.

Sometimes trunks or limbs bucked into sections longer than stove length can be lifted onto a sawbuck. This makes the final bucking much easier.

Splitting

Green wood splits much more easily than seasoned wood, so the task should be done as soon as possible after bucking. Split all pieces 6 inches in diameter or larger to speed seasoning, but make sure split pieces will fit in the stove. When splitting, use an anchored chopping block or a stump larger in diameter than the largest piece to be split. Splitting pieces directly on the ground is not a good idea, because the ground absorbs much of the energy of your swing and the dirt will quickly dull your ax or maul.

Relatively small pieces may be split with an ax; for medium to large pieces, use a 6 to 10-pound maul. Extremely large or difficult-to-split pieces may require the use of two or more wedges and a sledge hammer, or a power splitter (available at tool rental agencies). Splitting tools appear in the drawing on the facing page. Actual sizes of pieces that can be split with these tools will depend on the moisture content and grain pattern of the wood.

When using a maul or ax, look for radial cracks in the ends of the pieces. These usually provide a headstart on a clean split. A direct blow is more efficient than an angular one, so you should swing the maul perpendicular to the end of the piece you're splitting. For greater accuracy, center your body in front of the target spot and swing the ax or maul down directly in front of you, rather than to one side. One trick used to make a clean split with an ax or maul is to twirl or rotate the handle slightly the moment the cutting edge contacts the wood. Getting the hang of this trick takes practice, but once you have it down, it will make your splitting job much easier.

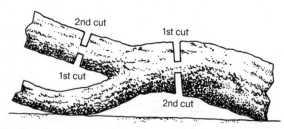

For free lengths, *start cut underneath, finish from top. Reverse procedure for lengths supported by limbs.*

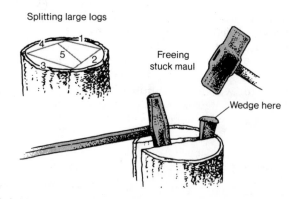

Splitting large logs

Freeing stuck maul

Wedge here

Split *four edges from large logs, then split through center (left). Drive wedge into crack to free stuck maul (right).*

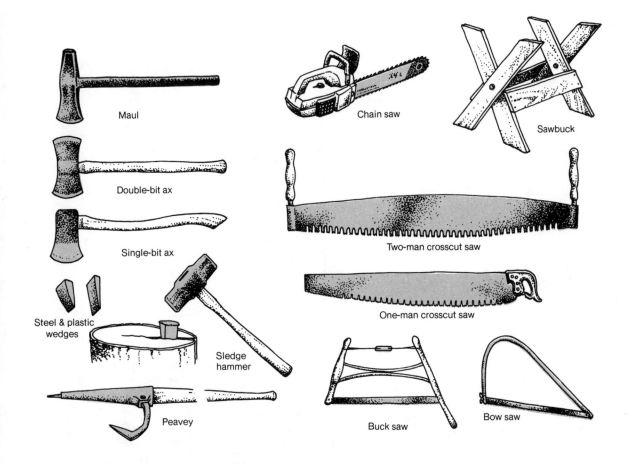

Maul

Chain saw

Sawbuck

Double-bit ax

Single-bit ax

Two-man crosscut saw

Steel & plastic wedges

Sledge hammer

One-man crosscut saw

Peavey

Buck saw

Bow saw

If the maul or ax gets stuck—even Paul Bunyan got his ax stuck occasionally—pound a wedge in the crack to release the tool (see drawing on page 86). Continue driving the wedge with a sledge hammer or the blunt side of the maul until the wood splits; but never use an ax to drive wedges. Also, never try to split large pieces directly in half—first split away the edges, then split through the remaining chunk.

Stacking and seasoning

Once the wood is cut and split into stove-sized pieces, it must be stacked and stored for seasoning. Seasoning times for different wood species will vary, but in general, 9 months to a year is enough to bring most woods to ideal dryness. If wood is stored much longer than 2 years, though, it will begin to decay, thus losing much of its heating value.

Stacking methods. For wood to season properly, it should be stacked off the ground and kept under cover during rain and snow seasons. To keep wood off the ground, stack it on parallel poles or stringers or rows of concrete blocks. Poles or stringers should be of a decay-resistant wood, such as redwood or red cedar, or be treated with a wood preservative to

prevent rot. Elevating the poles or stringers on bricks or blocks also helps prevent decay and allows air circulation under the pile to speed seasoning.

There are two stacking methods: parallel and crisscross. Both are shown in the drawing below. The parallel stack is the more compact of the two, though the crisscross method, with more rapid air circulation through the stack, speeds seasoning.

With either method, pieces having bark should be placed on top, bark-side up, since bark repels water better than wood does. Stacks should not exceed 5 feet in height, and stacks higher than 3 feet should have end braces. On the next page are plans for building end braces, along with designs for simple woodsheds.

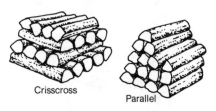

Crisscross

Parallel

Stacking *can be done two ways—crisscross (left) speeds drying, parallel (right) saves space.*

Three wood storage ideas

End frames

These easy-to-make redwood or cedar end frames can corral an unruly woodpile of practically any size. They work on the same principle as expandable bookends: as the wood stack grows or diminishes, you just move the end frames closer together or farther apart to accommodate it. The weight of the logs anchors the frames at the ends of the stack. Don't lay the logs between end frames directly on the ground; instead, set them on redwood or cedar 2 by 4 runners between frames.

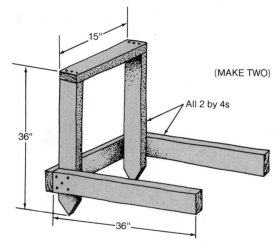

15"

36"

36"

(MAKE TWO)

All 2 by 4s

House-attached woodshed

Designed to hold about a cord of wood, this shelter utilizes an existing house wall for much of its support and to enclose its backside. Be sure to use only redwood or cedar heartwood or pressure-treated lumber in direct contact with the ground.

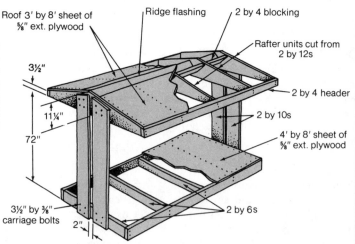

2 by 6 ledger bolted to wall   Flashing

2 by 6 rafters

4' x 8' sheet of ⅝" ext. plywood

Extra 2 by 6 at ends, flush with roof

78"

93½"

2 by 6 header

2 by 4 plate

2 by 4 stringers

2 by 6 block

2 by 4 double studs in front

2 by 4 back stud bolted to wall

Plywood or fiberglass cover on sides is optional

Freestanding wood shelter

This freestanding firewood shelter loads from either side and can contain a full cord. It's surprisingly easy to build from standard lumber and plywood. Where wood is in direct contact with the ground, be sure to use only cedar or redwood heartwood or pressure-treated lumber. For full stability, this shelter requires at least a partial load of wood.

Roof 3' by 8' sheet of ⅝" ext. plywood

Ridge flashing

2 by 4 blocking

Rafter units cut from 2 by 12s

3½"

2 by 4 header

11¼"

2 by 10s

72"

4' by 8' sheet of ⅝" ext. plywood

3½" by ⅜" carriage bolts

2"

2 by 6s

The Other Woodburners

If you are a dedicated wood burner, you may want to go beyond space heating and consider central heating, water heating, and cooking with wood. There are special variants of the basic wood stove that are designed for just these special purposes. This section describes these other woodburners and explains their applications. It also considers the freestanding fireplace, which combines some of the elements of both wood stoves and built-in fireplaces.

Wood-fired central heating

If wood is plentiful in your area, why not consider a wood-burning furnace? Like coal, wood is a solid fuel, and the market offers many efficient, central heating units designed to burn wood.

Wood furnaces differ from conventional furnaces only in the type of fuel they consume. Many wood furnaces are simply large wood stoves with sheet metal jackets designed to collect the heat and distribute it through duct work (see drawing, below). Some use elaborate heat exchangers to boost their capacity. Others use hot water as a heat transfer medium. On these units, the firebox is surrounded by a water jacket. Heated water is pumped, or it flows by natural convection, from the furnace through pipes to radiators.

Heating capacity varies widely among wood-burning furnaces. Units range from small models that produce about double the heat of a large wood stove to industrial models that produce 1.2 million BTUs per hour and burn two cords of wood a day.

The furnace may burn only wood, or it may have an additional burner designed to use gas or oil. The gas or oil burner on the unit is usually used as a backup to the wood fire. There are also wood furnaces designed as simple add-ons to conventional furnaces, a very economical method of increasing the flexibility of existing systems. The drawings on the next page show typical installations.

Is it for you?

Even if you have a plentiful wood supply, there are other factors you should consider before choosing a wood furnace. The cost of a wood-fired unit is high, perhaps twice that of a gas or oil furnace; and the multi-fuel feature may double the cost again. A high-priced wood furnace may not prove cost-effective, especially in small homes.

In many cases, wood stoves in one or two rooms might do the job more efficiently than a central furnace, especially if the house is well-insulated. Don't forget wood furnaces naturally consume more wood than wood stoves: they have the job of heating the whole house. It might also be less costly to upgrade the insulation in a drafty house rather than compensate for its leaks with a powerful central heater.

A new chimney may be required for a wood furnace, and that is another cost factor. Wood furnaces require Class A chimneys, either lined masonry or factory-built, all-fuel types; and in some cases these may be prohibitively expensive or difficult to adapt to an existing structure.

Wood furnaces are usually thermostatically controlled, but there is a great deal more to operating them than a simple check of the dial now and then. You will have to stoke a wood furnace at least once each day, and more likely twice. It will also need

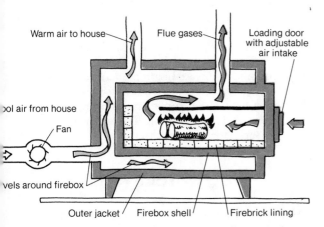

Warm air to house — Flue gases — Loading door with adjustable air intake

Cool air from house

Fan

Air travels around firebox

Outer jacket / Firebox shell / Firebrick lining

Forced-air wood-burning furnace *is essentially a wood stove within a steel jacket. The jacket confines radiant heat, directs air to the house.*

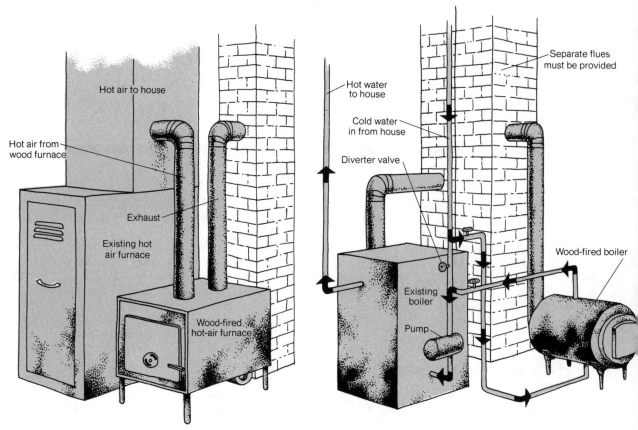

Labels in illustration:

Hot air to house

Hot air from wood furnace

Exhaust

Existing hot air furnace

Wood-fired hot-air furnace

Separate flues must be provided

Hot water to house

Cold water in from house

Diverter valve

Existing boiler

Pump

Wood-fired boiler

Add-on furnace or boiler *takes over heating chores from the conventional furnace or boiler. Conventional unit then becomes a backup in the home heating system.*

cleaning, perhaps once a month. The chimney should be inspected on a regular basis, especially if the furnace has been operating at a low level. Creosote is an almost certain by-product of wood-burning, and furnaces burn lots of wood. And because they burn lots of wood, it is crucial to locate a reliable source for the wood (see "A Woodchopper's guide," page 83).

Also, be sure to check the codes in your area. Not all furnaces are legal in all areas. As of this writing, no multi-fuel unit has a U.L. listing, and some codes may prohibit their installation.

Furnace location

Wood furnaces are much bulkier than their fossil-fuel counterparts. The fuel is also bulky and the furnace needs to be tended several times a day, so ease of access is important both for loading and cleanout. A basement location is ideal; it gives you the option of circulating the heat by natural convection, and it usually provides ample space for wood storage and easy cleaning of the furnace. The next best location is an outbuilding or garage attached to a wall of the house; but you will have to install blowers or pumps to circulate the hot air or water. Remember, too, that

the furnace will require a Class A chimney (see above), and this may also affect furnace placement.

Circulation

Wood furnaces are adaptable to either passive or active circulation. They can duplicate the gentle, slow heat of the passive "gravity" furnaces, found in many older homes, by allowing heat to rise naturally from floor to floor. Or they can provide active circulation by using blowers and ducts to achieve the rapid temperature rise and even heating of all corners of a room usually associated with modern forced-air central heating systems. A wood furnace can also supply hot-water heat, either convective or pumped. In addition, your system should include efficient return of cool air (or water) to the furnace.

Hot-water systems

Many stoves and furnaces are designed to heat water; others can be easily adapted to this purpose. Heat is usually transferred to the water by means of a water coil or manifold in the firebox or flue. Properly designed, such a system can easily provide most or all of a home's hot water needs during the months the stove or furnace is in operation.

For intermittent-demand situations, such as in a cabin or vacation home, wood-fired water heaters are available. These units have small fireboxes capable of heating a limited amount of water to a high temperature very quickly. The heaters are not intended to meet the demands of an open tap for very long, but they will provide for short showers and dish washing. These heaters are insulated and will not radiate much heat—an advantage on hot summer days. If a wood-fired system is used in conjunction with a conventional gas or electric water heater, year-round operation is possible. This combination can provide good capacity and low gas and electric bills, in addition to a year-round supply of hot water. There is also a trend toward solar/wood systems that promises economical year-round water heating.

Locating the coil

If your stove or furnace already has a hot water system, or if the manufacturer provides an add-on kit, you can skip this section. If not, you will have to decide where to locate the hot water coil or manifold, which can be placed in or on the stove or its flue. The three factors to consider are ease of installation, heat transfer efficiency, and maintenance.

Firebox coils. The best location is in the firebox because it is the source of heat and will cause the fewest maintenance problems. Temperatures in the firebox are so high that any creosote deposits are burned off during the normal operation of the stove. However, firebox mounting will require that you cut two holes in your stove—easy enough if your stove is made of steel, but best left to a skilled metalworker if it is iron.

Flue pipe coils. These installations are the easiest, but they do have some serious shortcomings. If you have an airtight stove, the coil should not be installed in the flue. Flue gas temperatures in an airtight stove are already too low for best heating, and the coil will further cool the flue, perhaps to the point of impairing the stove's draft. Also, a flue pipe coil accumulates creosote deposits: the coil's cool surface causes condensation of the tars that form creosote. These creosote deposits also tend to insulate the coil and reduce heat transfer efficiency.

Exterior coils. Installing these on either the flue or firebox will avoid the necessity of drilling holes and the problem of creosote deposits. But these exterior coils have comparatively poor heat transfer efficiency.

Materials. Coils and manifolds can be made of either copper tubing or iron pipe. Copper doesn't rust, is easily formed, and has very good heat-transfer efficiency; but it is delicate. If copper tubing is installed in the firebox, care must be taken when loading the stove to avoid crushing. Iron is much more rugged, but care must be taken with the necessary joints—a qualified plumber should do the job.

Many old stoves and kitchen ranges had "water backs"—cast-iron tanks built into their fireboxes. A modern adaptation of this old idea uses a steel jacket containing inlet and outlet pipes. Designed for firebox mounting, this unit has only two connections, heats effectively, and is extremely rugged.

Circulation

Circulation of water through the heating coil and into the storage tank is accomplished either passively (by natural convection) or actively (by means of pumps).

A passive or convective system is quite simple. The heated water naturally rises through the coil and into the top of the tank. Cooling, the water sinks to the bottom of the tank and back to the heating coil (see drawing, below). This is less efficient than an active system with its pump that moves a high volume of water rapidly. But what is lacking in efficiency is balanced by the gain in safety. Because there is no pump to malfunction, there is also no need to worry about a power failure that would keep the water from moving.

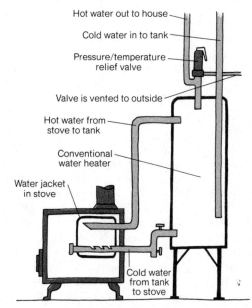

Hot water out to house
Cold water in to tank
Pressure/temperature relief valve
Valve is vented to outside
Hot water from stove to tank
Conventional water heater
Water jacket in stove
Cold water from tank to stove

In passive system, *water circulates by natural convection. Cold water sinks to bottom of tank, runs into water jacket in stove, and is heated there. Heated water rises out of stove and into top of tank, ready for use. Tank must be at least at the same level or slightly higher than stove; hot water from stove to tank must flow continuously upward with no dips to interrupt flow.*

If you opt for convective circulation, preferable for simplicity and safety as we've mentioned, the storage tank should be located near the stove and at the same level, or a little higher.

Active systems (see drawing, below), circulating water by means of a pump, move more water than convective systems and allow for more flexibility in locating the tank. But they are also more expensive, more complex, and involve more complicated safety precautions (see "Safety," below). Whether you elect an active or a passive system, be sure to consult a qualified heating engineer who knows local code requirements.

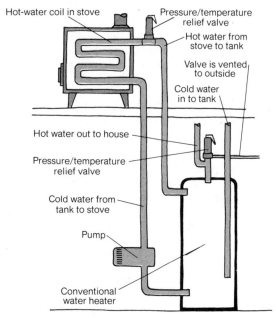

In active system, *pump circulates water between stove and tank, permitting placement of tank below stove.*

Safety

Safety is always a major consideration in hot water systems because hot water, when it becomes steam, produces extreme expansion and great pressure. Wood stoves heat water any time the stove is fired, and supply can occasionally outstrip demand. Thus, water in the storage tank will continue to heat, regardless of whether the water is actually being used. If water is allowed to sit in the coil, a steam explosion will occur; it is imperative to keep the water moving through the stove coil. All systems should have at least one automatic pressure/temperature relief valve.

From these considerations, it is obvious that safety precautions, such as proper location of pressure/temperature relief valves, are of paramount importance. The drawings above and on page 91 show typical locations of safety valves, but be sure to work with a qualified installer when designing your system.

Cooking on your wood stove or range

From the smallest box stove to the most elaborate antique range, almost all wood stoves can be used for some kind of cooking. Most small stoves can boil water and make toast; for the more ambitious, there are complete wood ranges that will also broil and bake.

You have to master fire building and control first, then you're ready to try cooking. And cooking on a wood stove offers its own unique rewards and subtle pleasures—all in exchange for just a little extra work and acquired skill.

Fire control

Learning to build and control the fire is very intimidating for prospective "wood cooks," but it is an essentially simple skill. Have light kindling and pine available for fast, hot fires; keep well-seasoned hardwood in readiness for the glowing coals needed for broiling and baking. You will find it helpful to split both kinds of wood into smaller sizes than you might ordinarily use for heating. This will enable you to start and control your fire more readily because the smaller pieces will catch fire and burn down more quickly than large pieces.

Once the fire is burning, temperature is adjusted by means of the stove's draft controls and damper. Control for most cooking is quite simple, but you will find that learning to "fine tune" your fire is the key to successful baking.

Stove-top cooking

The simplest operation is boiling water, and a teakettle gently simmering on the back of the stove is a natural. The stove will keep water warm or boil it, depending on the kettle's position. Move it over the fire for rapid heating, or place it to the rear for gentle simmering. If your kettle fits into one of the cookrings found on many cooktops, your stove will boil water rapidly. A kettle of boiling water also humidifies the room, a bonus feature in many climates.

Wood stoves make excellent toast—and nothing beats the old-fashioned toaster rack. Or simply place a piece of bread on the cooking surface and flip it over when the first side is done.

Pan frying is equally easy and best accomplished over the hottest part of the fire. You can even use the surface of the stove itself, but cleanup may be messy.

If you're a wok enthusiast, you'll enjoy using one on your wood stove. Woks were originally developed for use with small charcoal stoves: a hole in the stove top was designed to accept the bottom of the wok, putting it in direct contact with the flames. This led to the development of stir-fry cooking where the

Box stove *with cooktop has removable pothole lids for faster heating. Raised edge keeps pots from sliding off.*

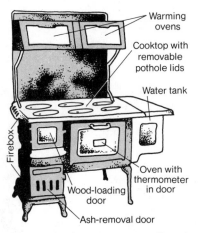

Warming ovens

Cooktop with removable pothole lids

Water tank

Firebox

Oven with thermometer in door

Wood-loading door

Ash-removal door

Turn-of-the-century range *is still made today; original molds are used.*

Antique range *has same features as turn-of-the-century range, but with ornate filigree and much nickel plating added. Properly maintained, such stoves work as well as they ever did and add charm as well as function to the kitchen.*

Scandinavian cookstove *is compact, efficient. Firebox is at left, small oven on right.*

Modern gas/wood range *combines the best of both worlds. Wood firebox and cooktop are at left, conventional oven and surface units at right.*

food is moved in and out of the intensely hot area at the bottom of the wok.

If your wood stove has a pothole lid, try taking it out and setting your wok into the opening. This closely duplicates the original Chinese arrangement and is excellent for stir-frying food. If you don't have a cook-top opening, place the wok on the hot top of the stove and it will work nearly as well.

Cast-iron cookware is best for use with wood stoves; its even heat distribution helps insure against hot spots. Another hint—Give your warm stove-top a swipe with a waxy-type breadwrapper (or wax paper if you're not a purist) and it will gleam.

Broiling & baking

Broiling involves more fire management than stovetop cooking, but it is still quite simple. Be sure you have an even bed of hardwood coals. You can broil directly on the coals or you can use a firebox rack. Racks are supplied with many ranges, and some ranges have special side doors that provide easy access to the firebox. If you elect to broil right on the coals, be sure to turn the meat frequently. A light brushing with oil will help to prevent burning.

Baking provides the real test for the wood cook, however, since temperature regulation is so important. Wood-burning cookstoves have dampers that direct hot gases from the firebox to underneath the oven, and block their usual passage over it. These

dampers control the oven temperature, and mastery of them is a real skill. Old-time cooks knew their oven's heat by touch or instinct, but you'd best use an oven thermometer. And because one oven wall may be hotter than the others, it may also be necessary to rotate the food in the oven occasionally. It's mostly a matter of practicing the use of the oven damper, flue damper, and draft controls. Do this and you'll be able to hold an even temperature over the entire baking period.

All this may sound like a lot of work, but it does have its rewards. Experienced wood cooks will tell you that anything baked in a wood oven tastes better. Wood ovens aren't vented, so the aroma stays in and enhances the flavor of the food.

Special features

Wood ranges do offer features not found on gas or electric stoves. The warming ovens at the top of many wood ranges have a multitude of uses. Besides keeping dinner warm, they are excellent for raising bread dough and drying anything from fruit to soggy mittens. Available accessories for some models include hot water coils and reservoirs, drying racks, and glass doors.

Some woodburning ranges are designed to heat the kitchen; others are insulated to retain heat and prevent radiation. Choosing between the two is largely a matter of climate. If summers are warm in your area and you plan to use the stove all year, you will need an insulated model. In cooler climates, an uninsulated stove in a centrally located kitchen can heat the whole house.

Cleaning & safety

The complicated flue passages of a wood range will accumulate soot and creosote. Allowing these deposits to build up can create a safety problem; if your range is in daily use, you should plan to clean these passages once a month. And regular cleaning will pay off in operation: creosote and soot are insulators so a regular cleaning will improve your range's efficiency.

Freestanding fireplaces

The freestanding metal fireplace has become a modern classic. Available in a wide variety of shapes, colors, and sizes, it has a number of advantages over masonry fireplaces. Chimney and hearth installation is similar to that of a wood stove (see "Installing Your Stove," pages 66-77), but your local building codes may impose different installation requirements. So check to be sure you are in conformance. Also be sure to obtain a building permit before installation; any kind of fireplace is considered a permanent addition.

Efficiency

All freestanding fireplaces are vastly more efficient than masonry units, and some glass-enclosed models are nearly as efficient as nonairtight stoves. Their large hoods and stacks radiate heat rapidly, making them ideal for small cabins and vacation homes. Some models have masses of refractory material in their bases and hoods; once heated, they continue warming a room even after the fire has died down.

Fire control

The flue damper that comes with most units can compensate to some extent for the lack of draft controls on open-hearth models. This allows you to slow the fire, thus reducing the amount of warm room air drawn up the chimney. Nevertheless, the metal surfaces continue to radiate heat into the room at about the same rate, regardless of the damper setting.

Flexibility

Designing around freestanding fireplaces is easy. Options on color and shape make them adaptable to almost any situation, and their minimum silhouettes allow you to position them in front of windows so that seating can be arranged to focus on the view as well as the fire. Circular models permit central placement, ideal for heat radiation and a view of the fire from all points in the room.

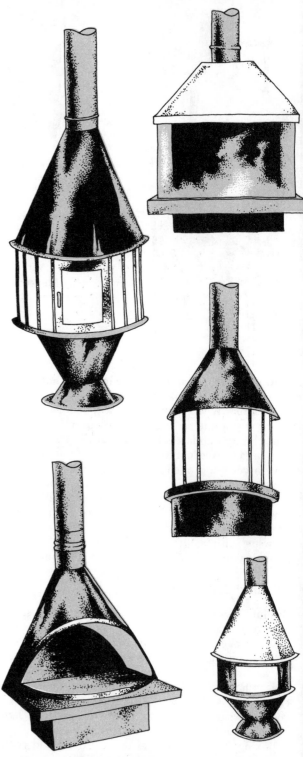

Freestanding fireplaces *come in myriad shapes, sizes, and colors. They offer unique opportunities to the decorator but cannot match the efficiency of a wood stove. Still, they may be the solution to your design problem.*

Wood Heat Terms: A Glossary

Air inlet. Opening in a stove that allows combustion air to enter. Also referred to as dampers, these openings are adjustable to control the amount of air feeding the fire.

Available heat. Actual amount of heat given off by various kinds of wood when burned in a stove; the amount depends on the species of wood, its moisture content, and the heating efficiency of the stove. *See also* Potential heat.

Backpuffing. Emission of smoke through openings in the stove, caused by air flow reversal in the chimney. Backpuffing is a result of poor or insufficient draft.

Baffle. A plate or partition inside the stove used to direct the flow of combustion air, flames, or flue gases. A baffle is considered to increase a stove's heating efficiency.

BTU or British Thermal Unit. Basic heat measurement, equivalent to amount of heat needed to raise 1 pound of water 1°F.

Chimney connection. Assembly consisting of stovepipe, pipe elbows, and related components used to connect stove to outside chimney.

Circulating stove. Stove with an outer metal jacket surrounding the firebox. Vents in the top and bottom of the jacket allow air to circulate through the intervening air space by convection.

Coal scuttle or hod. Bucket used to load coal-burning stoves, also handy for removing ashes from wood stoves and for storing wood near the stove.

Coaling process. The stage in wood combustion when charcoal ignites and burns, reducing itself to ash.

Conduction. Transference of heat through a solid material. Materials such as cast iron and steel conduct heat better than materials like wood.

Convection. Transference of heat through air or liquids; for example, heated air rises and is displaced by cooler air, setting up convective currents that transfer that heat.

Creosote. Tarry, flammable substance produced by the condensation of gases emitted from burning wood. Its buildup in flue pipes and chimneys creates a fire hazard.

Damper. Adjustable device located either on the stove (*see* Air inlet) or in the flue pipe above the stove, to control draft and therefore the burning rate.

Draft. Airflow through stove and chimney when fire is burning; also used to describe airflow pattern within stove: updraft, downdraft, S-draft, diagonal draft, cross draft.

Firebrick. Brick made of fire clay, used to line fireboxes in stoves and furnaces to extend their life.

Firestop spacer. Noncombustible spacer (usually sheet metal) used to provide clearance between chimney pipe and combustible walls or ceilings.

Flue collar. Collar around flue vent on stove that fits into or over flue pipe.

Flue gases. Flammable gases produced by burning wood. These gases will ignite and burn at temperatures above 1100°F/600°C.

Flue liner. Fire clay tiles used to line masonry chimneys.

Flue pipe. *See* Single wall stovepipe.

Furnace cement. Noncombustible caulking compound used to seal joints or cracks in wood stoves and furnaces.

Green wood. Unseasoned wood, or wood freshly cut from a live tree.

Heat exchanger. Heat-recovery device installed on or in the stove or its flue pipe to extract additional heat.

Heating capacity. Maximum heat output of a stove when operated under safe conditions; heating capacity is expressed in BTUs per hour.

Heating efficiency. Stove's ability to convert wood's potential heat into usable heat; for example, a stove that converts half of wood's potential heat into usable heat has a heating efficiency of 50 percent.

Heat mass. *See* Thermal mass.

Insulated pipe. Multiwalled chimney pipe used in wood stove installations to prevent heat loss and maintain proper flue temperatures for sufficient draft.

Insulative stoveboard. Noncombustible hearth material used to cover combustible walls and floors so that stove clearances to these surfaces may be reduced.

Mica. Translucent mineral capable of resisting high temperatures, used in stoves to allow fire viewing. On most new stoves, tempered glass has replaced mica for this purpose.

Open stove. Stove with one end open, or having large doors that may be opened for fire viewing.

Peavey. Tool used for rolling large logs or tree trunks; a peavey is pictured on page 87.

Potential heat. Maximum amount of heat available from any given species of wood. Potential heat figures for various woods (in BTUs) are determined by burning the wood at zero percent moisture content under laboratory conditions.

Radiant stove. Stove that heats primarily by radiation.

Radiation. Transmission of heat in the form of infrared rays; radiant heat.

Seasoned wood. Wood that has been air dried to the point that its moisture content remains constant with that of the surrounding atmosphere; also wood suitable for burning.

Secondary combustion. Burning of flue gases inside a stove. Both oxygen and high temperatures (above 1100°F/600°C) must be present for secondary combustion to occur.

Secondary air inlets. Air inlets on a stove, designed to provide sufficient oxygen for secondary combustion to take place.

Single wall stovepipe. Metal pipe, usually 24 gauge, used to connect the stove to the outside chimney; also referred to as flue pipe or chimney connector pipe.

Stove black (polish). Compound available in liquid or paste for polishing black cast-iron stoves.

Tempered glass. Glass that has been tempered to resist high temperatures; used in stoves to allow a view of the fire.

Thermal mass. Material or mass of sufficient size and density to have heat storage capabilities; for example, thick-bodied stoves and massive hearths have sufficient thermal mass to store heat.

Zero-clearance stoves (and heaters). Stoves designed to be placed directly against a combustible wall or floor.

Index

Photographers

Edward Bigelow: 34 top, 40 top right, 41 bottom, 43 bottom, 44 top, 45 bottom right, 47 bottom, 48, 51 top and right, 52 bottom, 53, 54, 55 bottom, 56 left, 57 right, 60 bottom, 61, back cover bottom. **Steve W. Marley:** 36 top, 38 bottom, 40 top right, 41 top, 43 top left. **Jack McDowell:** 34 left, 35 top left and right, bottom right, 36 bottom left, 37 bottom right, 42 top, 43 top right, 47 top, 49 top, 57 left, 58, 59, 60 top, 62 top and bottom right, 63, back cover top. **Rob Super:** 33, 34 bottom right, 35 bottom left, 36 bottom right, 37 top and bottom left, 38 top, 39, 40 bottom, 42 bottom, 44 bottom, 45 top and bottom left, 46, 49 bottom, 50, 51 bottom left, 52 top, 55 top, 56 right, 62 bottom left.

6748